2ND EDITION

Birds *of* Maine

Field Guide

Stan Tekiela

PUBLICATIONS
Adventure
an imprint of **AdventureKEEN**

Edited by Sandy Livoti, Brett Ortler, and Andrew Mollenkof

Cover, book design, and illustrations by Jonathan Norberg

Range maps produced by Anthony Hertzel

Cover photo: Common Yellowthroat by Stan Tekiela
All photos by Stan Tekiela except p. 296 (juvenile) by **Rick & Nora Bowers;** p. 290 (juvenile)
by **Phillippe Clement/shutterstock.com;** p. 242 (displaying) by **cliff collings/shutterstock.
com;** pp. 170 (displaying), 252 (displaying), 292 (in flight) by **Dudley Edmondson;** pp. 212
(female), 310 female by **Kevin T. Karlson;** pp. 44 (female), 282 (female), 318 (female) by
Maslowski Wildlife Productions; p. 33 (juvenile) by **Paul Reeves Photography/shutterstock.
com;** p. 290 (male) by **Piotr Poznan/shutterstock.com;** p. 236 (female) by **RLHambley/shut-
terstock.com;** p. 33 (male) by **Amit Satiya/shutterstock.com;** pp. 40 (juvenile), 154 (both
juveniles); 254 (juvenile), 256 (in-flight juvenile) by **Brian K. Wheeler;** pp. 194 (female), 250,
258 (female), 300 (in flight), 306 (female) by **Jim Zipp.**

10 9 8 7 6 5 4 3 2 1

Birds of Maine Field Guide
First Edition 2002
Second Edition 2023
Copyright © 2002 and 2023 by Stan Tekiela
Published by Adventure Publications
An imprint of AdventureKEEN
310 Garfield Street South
Cambridge, Minnesota 55008
(800) 678-7006
www.adventurepublications.net
All rights reserved
Printed in China
Cataloging-in-Publication data is available from the Library of Congress
ISBN 978-1-64755-368-5 (pbk.); ISBN 978-1-64755-369-2 (ebook)

TABLE OF CONTENTS

WHAT'S NEW?

It is hard to believe that it's been more than 20 years since the debut of *Birds of Maine Field Guide*. This critically acclaimed field guide has helped countless people identify and enjoy the birds that we love. Now, in this expanded third edition, *Birds of Maine Field Guide* has many new and exciting changes and a fresh look, while retaining the same familiar, easy-to-use format.

To help you identify even more birds in Maine, I have added 6 new species and more than 150 new color photographs. All of the range maps have been meticulously reviewed, and many updates have been made to reflect the ever-changing movements of the birds.

Everyone's favorite section, "Stan's Notes," has been expanded to include even more natural history information. "Compare" sections have been updated to help ensure that you correctly identify your bird, and additional feeder information has been added to help with bird feeding. I hope you will enjoy this great new edition as you continue to learn about and appreciate our Maine birds!

WHY WATCH BIRDS IN MAINE?

Millions of people have discovered bird feeding. It's a simple and enjoyable way to bring the beauty of birds closer to your home. Watching birds at your feeder and listening to them often leads to a lifetime pursuit of bird identification. The *Birds of Maine Field Guide* is for those who want to identify the common birds of Maine.

There are over 1,100 species of birds found in North America. In Maine alone there have been more than 460 kinds of birds recorded through the years. These bird sightings were diligently recorded by hundreds of bird watchers and became part of the official state record. From these records, I've chosen 125 of the most common and easily seen birds of Maine to include in this field guide.

Bird watching, often called birding, is one of the most popular activities in America. Its outstanding appeal in Maine is due, in part, to an unusually rich and abundant birdlife. Why are there so many birds? One reason is open space. Maine is over 33,000 square miles (85,800 sq. km), making it the thirty-ninth-largest state. Maine is the largest of the New England states, having an area that is nearly equal to all other New England states combined. Despite its large size, only about 1.3 million people call Maine home. On average, that is only 44 people per square mile (17 per sq. km). Most of these people are located in and around only three major cities.

Open space is not the only reason there is such an abundance of birds—it's also the diversity of habitat. This state can be divided into three main regions—the Seaboard Lowland, New England Upland, and the White Mountains.

The Seaboard Lowland is a coastal border that is 30 to 60 miles (48 to 97 km) wide. This is a region with pine-covered, gently rolling hills and isolated rock outcroppings. It is also an area where fresh water flows out of the land from rivers and mixes with saltwater from the ocean, creating a rich habitat known as an estuary. This habitat supports a very diverse bird population that includes Ring-billed Gulls, Ospreys and many shorebird species such as Spotted Sandpipers.

Maine has 228 miles (367 km) of coastline. Including the bays, inlets, river estuaries, and islands, there is more than 3,000 miles (4,830 km) of coastal surface. These coastal areas are home to many ocean-loving birds such as the colony-nesting Common Tern, Arctic Tern, and Ruddy Turnstone. Maine also has many freshwater and saltwater marshes. The marshes are great places to see water birds such as Great Blue Herons.

Inland from the coastal plain is a region called the New England Upland. The rolling topography here is covered with forests and dotted with clear lakes and rivers. This region offers habitat for Wood Ducks, Ring-necked Ducks, and other waterfowl. It is a great place to see an altogether different group of birds than those found in the Seaboard Lowland.

The White Mountains in the western portion of the state add to the great diversity of birds in Maine. This mountainous habitat is entirely different from habitats seen elsewhere in the state. Birds that are more characteristic of the northern forest, such as the Red-breasted Nuthatch and Dark-eyed Junco, are found here.

Finally, varying weather in Maine attracts many different birds. High elevations in the western part of the state are much colder and snowier than habitats near the ocean. Winter temperatures across Maine stay below freezing during winter, while summers can be hot and humid.

Whether watching a nesting colony of herons and egrets near the Atlantic Ocean or welcoming back the hummingbirds in spring, bird watchers enjoy variety and excitement in the birds of Maine as each season turns to the next.

OBSERVATION STRATEGIES:
TIPS FOR IDENTIFYING BIRDS

Identifying birds isn't as difficult as you might think. By simply following a few basic strategies, you can increase your chances of successfully identifying most birds that you see. One of the first and easiest things to do when you see a new bird is to note **its color**. This field guide is organized by color, so simply turn to the right color section to find it.

Next, note the **size of the bird.** A strategy to quickly estimate size is to compare different birds. Pick a small, a medium, and a large bird. Select an American Robin as the medium bird. Measured from bill tip to tail tip, a robin is 10 inches (25 cm). Now select two other birds, one smaller and one larger. Good choices are a House Sparrow, at about 6 inches (15 cm), and an American Crow, around 18 inches (45 cm). When you see a species you don't know, you can now quickly ask yourself, "Is it larger than a sparrow but smaller than a robin?" When you look in your field guide to identify your bird, you would check the species that are roughly 6–10 inches (15–25 cm). This will help to narrow your choices.

Next, note the **size, shape, and color of the bill.** Is it long or short, thick or thin, pointed or blunt, curved or straight? Seed-eating birds, such as Northern Cardinals, have bills that are thick and strong enough to crack even the toughest seeds. Birds that sip nectar, such as Ruby-throated Hummingbirds, need long, thin bills to reach deep into flowers. Hawks and owls tear their prey with very sharp, curving bills. Sometimes, just noting the bill shape can help you decide whether the bird is a woodpecker, finch, grosbeak, blackbird, or bird of prey.

Next, take a look around and note the **habitat** in which you see the bird. Is it wading in a marsh? Walking along a riverbank? Soaring in the sky? Is it perched high in the trees or hopping along the forest floor? Because of diet and habitat preferences, you'll often see robins hopping on the ground but not usually eating seeds at a feeder. Or you'll see a Blue Jay sitting on a tree branch but not climbing headfirst down the trunk, like a White-breasted Nuthatch would.

Noticing **what the bird is eating** will give you another clue to help you identify the species. Feeding is a big part of any bird's life. Fully one-third of all bird activity revolves around searching for food, catching prey and eating. While birds don't always follow all the rules of their diet, you can make some general assumptions. Northern Flickers, for instance, feed on ants and other insects, so you wouldn't expect to see them visiting a seed feeder. Other birds, such as Barn and Tree Swallows, eat flying insects and spend hours swooping and diving to catch a meal.

Sometimes you can identify a bird by **the way it perches.** Body posture can help you differentiate between an American Crow and a Red-tailed Hawk, for example. Crows lean forward over their feet on a branch, while hawks perch in a vertical position. Consider posture the next time you see an unidentified large bird in a tree.

Birds in flight are harder to identify, but noting the **wing size and shape** will help. Wing size is in direct proportion to body size, weight, and type of flight. Wing shape determines whether the bird flies fast and with precision, or slowly and less precisely. Barn Swallows, for instance, have short, pointed wings that slice through the air, enabling swift, accurate flight. Turkey Vultures have long, broad wings for soaring on warm updrafts. House Finches have short, rounded wings, helping them to flit through thick tangles of branches.

Some bird species have a unique **pattern of flight** that can help in identification. American Goldfinches fly in a distinctive undulating pattern that makes it look like they're riding a roller coaster.

While it's not easy to make all of these observations in the short time you often have to watch a "mystery" bird, practicing these identification methods will greatly expand your birding skills. To further improve your skills, seek the guidance of a more experienced birder who can answer your questions on the spot.

BIRD BASICS

It's easier to identify birds and communicate about them if you know the names of the different parts of a bird. For instance, it's more effective to use the word "crest" to indicate the set of extra-long feathers on top of a Northern Cardinal's head than to try to describe it.

The following illustration points out the basic parts of a bird. Because it is a composite of many birds, it shouldn't be confused with any actual bird.

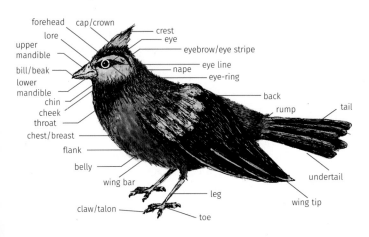

Bird Color Variables

No other animal has a color palette like a bird's. Brilliant blues, lemon yellows, showy reds, and iridescent greens are common in the bird world. In general, male birds are more colorful than their female counterparts. This helps males attract a mate, essentially saying, "Hey, look at me!" Color calls attention to a male's health as well. The better the condition of his feathers, the better his food source, territory and potential for mating.

When male and female birds of the same species don't look like each other, they are called sexually dimorphic, meaning "two forms." Dimorphic females often have a nondescript, dull color, as seen in Indigo Buntings. Muted tones not only help females hide during the weeks of motionless incubation but also draw less attention to them when they're out feeding or taking a break from the rigors of raising the young.

The males and females of some species, such as the Downy Woodpecker, Blue Jay, and Bald Eagle, look nearly identical. In woodpeckers, they are differentiated by only a red (sometimes yellow or black) mark; this mark may be on top of the head, on the face or nape, or just behind the bill.

During the first year, juvenile birds often look like their mothers. Since brightly colored feathers are used mainly for attracting a mate, young non-breeding males don't have a need for colorful plumage. It's not until the first spring molt (or several years later, depending on the species) that young males obtain their breeding colors.

Both breeding and winter plumages are the result of molting. Molting is the process of dropping old, worn feathers and replacing them with new ones. All birds molt, typically twice a year, with the spring molt usually occurring in late winter. At this time, most birds produce their brighter breeding plumage, which lasts throughout the summer.

Winter plumage is the result of the late-summer molt, which serves a couple of important functions. First, it adds feathers for warmth in the coming winter season. Second, in some species it produces feathers that tend to be drab in color, which helps to camouflage the birds and hide them from predators. The winter plumage of the male American Goldfinch, for example, is olive-brown, unlike its canary-yellow breeding color during summer. Luckily for us, some birds, such as the male Northern Cardinal, retain their bright summer colors all year long.

Bird Nests

Bird nests are a true feat of engineering. Imagine constructing a home that's strong enough to weather storms, large enough to hold your entire family, insulated enough to shelter them from cold and heat, and waterproof enough to keep out rain. Think about building it without blueprints or directions and using mainly your feet. Birds do this!

Before building, birds must select an appropriate site. In some species, such as the House Wren, the male picks out several potential sites and assembles small twigs in each. The "extra" nests, called dummy nests, discourage other birds from using any nearby cavities for their nests. The male takes the female around and shows her the choices. After choosing her favorite, she finishes the construction.

In other species, such as the Baltimore Oriole, the female selects the site and builds the nest, while the male offers an occasional suggestion. Each bird species has its own nest-building routine that is strictly followed.

As you can see in these illustrations, birds build a wide variety of nest types.

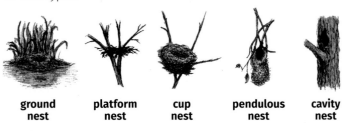

| ground nest | platform nest | cup nest | pendulous nest | cavity nest |

Nesting material often consists of natural items found in the immediate area. Most nests consist of plant fibers (such as bark from grapevines), sticks, mud, dried grass, feathers, fur, or soft, fuzzy tufts from thistle. Some birds, including Ruby-throated Hummingbirds, use spiderwebs to glue nest materials together.

Transportation of nesting material is limited to the amount a bird can hold or carry. Birds must make many trips afield to gather enough material to complete a nest. Most nests take four days or more, and hundreds, if not thousands, of trips to build.

A **ground nest** can be a mound of vegetation on the ground or in the water. It can also be just a simple shallow depression scraped out in earth, stones, or sand. Killdeer and Horned Larks scrape out ground nests without adding any nesting material.

The **platform nest** represents a much more complex type of construction. Typically built with twigs or sticks and branches, this nest forms a platform and has a depression in the center to nestle the eggs. Platform nests can be in trees; on balconies, cliffs, bridges, or man-made platforms; and even in flowerpots. They often provide space for the adventurous young and function as a landing platform for the parents.

Mourning Doves and herons don't anchor their platform nests to trees, so these can tumble from branches during high winds and storms. Hawks, eagles, ospreys, and other birds construct sturdier platform nests with large sticks and branches.

Other platform nests are constructed on the ground with mud, grass, and other vegetation from the area. Many waterfowl build platform nests on the ground near or in water. A **floating platform nest** moves with the water level, preventing the nest, eggs, and birds from being flooded.

Three-quarters of all songbirds construct a **cup nest,** which is a modified platform nest. The supporting platform is built first and attached firmly to a tree, shrub, or rock ledge, or the ground. Next, the sides are constructed with grass, small twigs, bark, or leaves, which are woven together and often glued with mud for added strength. The inner cup can be lined with down feathers, animal fur or hair, or soft plant materials and is contoured last.

The **pendulous nest** is an unusual nest that looks like a sock hanging from a branch. Attached to the end of small branches of trees, this unique nest is inaccessible to most predators and often waves wildly in a breeze.

Woven tightly with plant fibers, the pendulous nest is strong and watertight and takes up to a week to build. A small opening at the top or on the side allows parents access to the grass-lined interior. More commonly used by tropical birds, this complex nest has also been mastered by orioles and kinglets. It must be one heck of a ride to be inside one of these nests during a windy spring thunderstorm!

The **cavity nest** is used by many species of birds, most notably woodpeckers and Eastern Bluebirds. A cavity nest is often excavated from a branch or tree trunk and offers shelter from storms, sun, cold, and predators. A small entrance hole in a tree can lead to a nest chamber that is up to a safe 10 inches (25 cm) deep.

Typically made by woodpeckers, cavity nests are usually used only once by the builder. Nest cavities can be used for many subsequent years by such inhabitants as Wood Ducks, mergansers, and bluebirds. Kingfishers, on the other hand, can dig a tunnel up to 4 feet (1 m) long in a riverbank. The nest chamber at the end of the tunnel is already well insulated, so it's usually only sparsely lined.

One of the most clever of all nests is the **no nest,** or daycare nest. Parasitic birds, such as Brown-headed Cowbirds, don't build their own nests. Instead, the egg-laden female searches out the nest of another bird and sneaks in to lay an egg while the host mother isn't looking.

A mother cowbird wastes no energy building a nest only to have it raided by a predator. Laying her eggs in the nests of other birds transfers the responsibility of raising her young to the host. When she lays her eggs in several nests, the chances increase that at least one of her babies will live to maturity.

Who Builds the Nest?

Generally, the female bird constructs the nest. She gathers the materials and does the building, with an occasional visit from her mate to check on progress. In some species, both parents contribute equally to nest building. The male may forage for sticks, grass, or mud, but it is the female that often fashions the nest. Only rarely does a male build a nest by himself.

Fledging

Fledging is the time between hatching and flight, or leaving the nest. Some species of birds are **precocial,** meaning they leave the nest within hours of hatching, though it may be weeks before they can fly. This is common in waterfowl and shorebirds.

Baby birds that hatch naked and blind need to stay in the nest for a few weeks (these birds are **altricial**). Baby birds that are still in the nest are **nestlings.** Until birds start to fly, they are called **fledglings.**

Why Birds Migrate

Why do so many species of birds migrate? The short answer is simple: food. Birds migrate to locations with abundant food, as it is easier to breed where food is plentiful than where food is scarce. Rose-breasted Grosbeak, for instance, are **complete migrators** that fly from the tropics of Central and South America to nest in the forests of North America, where billions of newly hatched insects are available to feed to their young.

Other migrators, such as some birds of prey, migrate back to northern regions in spring. In these locations, they hunt mice, voles, and other small rodents that are beginning to breed.

Complete migrators have a set time and pattern of migration. Every year at nearly the same time, they head to a specific wintering ground. Complete migrators may travel great distances, sometimes 15,000 miles (24,100 km) or more in one year.

Complete migration doesn't necessarily mean flying from New York to a tropical destination. Dark-eyed Juncos, for example, are complete migrators that move from the far reaches of Canada to spend the winter here in cold and snowy New York. This trip is still considered complete migration.

Complete migrators have many interesting aspects. In spring, males often leave a few weeks before the females, arriving early to scope out possibilities for nesting sites and food sources, and to begin to defend territories. The females arrive several weeks later. In many species, the females and their young leave earlier in the fall, often up to four weeks before the adult males.

Other species, such as the American Goldfinch, are **partial migrators**. These birds usually wait until their food supplies dwindle before flying south. Unlike complete migrators, partial migrators move only far enough south, or sometimes east and west, to find abundant food. In some years it might be only a few hundred miles, while in other years it can be as much as a thousand. This kind of migration, dependent on weather and the availability of food, is sometimes called seasonal movement.

Unlike the predictable complete migrators or partial migrators, **irruptive migrators** can move every third to fifth year or, in some cases, in consecutive years. These migrations are triggered when times are tough and food is scarce. Red-breasted Nuthatches are irruptive migrators. They leave their normal northern range in search of more food or in response to overpopulation.

Many other birds don't migrate at all. Black-capped Chickadees, for example, are **non-migrators** that remain in their habitat all year long and just move around as necessary to find food.

How Birds Migrate

One of the many secrets of migration is fat. While most people are fighting the ongoing battle of the bulge, birds intentionally gorge themselves to gain as much fat as possible without losing the ability to fly. Fat provides the greatest amount of energy per unit of weight. In the same way that your car needs gas, birds are propelled by fat and stall without it.

During long migratory flights, fat deposits are used up quickly, and birds need to stop to refuel. This is when backyard bird feeding stations and undeveloped, natural spaces around our towns and cities are especially important. Some birds require up to 2–3 days of constant feeding to build their fat reserves before continuing their seasonal trip.

Many birds, such as most eagles, hawks, ospreys, falcons, and vultures, migrate during the day. Larger birds can hold more body fat, go longer without eating and take longer to migrate. These birds glide along on rising columns of warm air, called thermals, that hold them aloft while they slowly make their way north or south. They generally rest at night and hunt early in the morning before the sun has a chance to warm the land and create good soaring conditions. Daytime migrators use a combination of landforms, rivers, and the rising and setting sun to guide them in the right direction.

The majority of small birds, called **passerines,** migrate at night. Studies show that some use the stars to navigate. Others use the setting sun, and still others, such as pigeons, use Earth's magnetic field to guide them north or south.

While flying at night may not seem like a good idea, it's actually safer. First, there are fewer avian predators hunting for birds at night. Second, night travel allows time during the day to find food in unfamiliar surroundings. Third, wind patterns at night tend to be flat, or laminar. Flat winds don't have the turbulence of daytime winds and can help push the smaller birds along.

HOW TO USE THIS GUIDE

To help you quickly and easily identify birds, this field guide is organized by color. Refer to the color key on the first page, note the color of the bird, and turn to that section. For example, the male Rose-breasted Grosbeak is black-and-white with a red patch on his chest. Because the bird is mostly black-and-white, it will be found in the black-and-white section.

Each color section is also arranged by size, generally with the smaller birds first. Sections may also incorporate the average size in a range, which in some cases reflects size differences between male and female birds. Flip through the pages in the color section to find the bird. If you already know the name of the bird, check the index for the page number.

In some species, the male and female are very different in color. In others, the breeding and winter plumage colors differ. These species will have an inset photograph with a page reference and will be found in two color sections.

You will find a variety of information in the bird description sections. To learn more, turn to the sample on pp. 22–23.

Range Maps

Range maps are included for each bird. Colored areas indicate where the bird is frequently found. The colors represent the presence of a species during a specific season, not the density, or amount, of birds in the area. Green is used for summer, blue for winter, red for year-round, and yellow for migration.

While every effort has been made to depict accurate ranges, these are constantly in flux due to a variety of factors. Changing weather, habitat, species abundance, and availability of vital resources, such as food and water, can affect the migration and movement of local populations, causing birds to be found in areas that are atypical for the species. So please use the maps as intended—as general guides only.

female
p. 113

male

Common Name

Range Map   *Scientific name*   **Color Indicator**

YEAR-ROUND
SUMMER
MIGRATION
WINTER

Size: measurement is from head to tip of tail; wingspan may be listed as well

Male: brief description of the male bird; may include breeding, winter, or other plumages

Female: brief description of the female bird, which is sometimes different from the male

Juvenile: brief description of the juvenile bird, which often looks like the adult female

Nest: kind of nest the bird builds to raise its young; who builds it; number of broods per year

Eggs: number of eggs you might expect to see in a nest; color and marking

Incubation: average days the parents spend incubating the eggs; who does the incubation

Fledging: average days the young spend in the nest after hatching but before they leave the nest; who does the most "childcare" and feeding

Migration: type of migrator: complete (seasonal, consistent), partial (seasonal, destination varies), irruptive (unpredictable, depends on the food supply), or non-migrator

Food: what the bird eats most of the time (e.g., seeds, insects, fruit, nectar, small mammals, fish) and whether it typically comes to a bird feeder

Compare: notes about other birds that look similar and the pages on which they can be found; may include extra information to aid in identification

Stan's Notes: Interesting natural history information. This could be something to look or listen for or something to help positively identify the bird. Also includes remarkable features.

23

female
p. 131

male

Eastern Towhee
Pipilo erythrophthalmus

SUMMER

Size: 7–8" (18–20 cm)

Male: Mostly black with rusty-brown sides and a white belly. Long black tail with a white tip. Short, stout, pointed bill, and rich-red eyes. White wing patches flash in flight.

Female: similar to male but brown instead of black

Juvenile: light brown with a heavily streaked head, chest, and belly; long, dark tail with a white tip

Nest: cup; female builds; 2 broods per year

Eggs: 3–4; cream-white with brown markings

Incubation: 12–13 days; female incubates

Fledging: 10–12 days; male and female feed the young

Migration: complete, southern states, South America

Food: insects, seeds, fruit; visits ground feeders

Compare: The American Robin (p. 239) lacks the white belly. The Gray Catbird (p. 235) lacks the black head and rusty sides. The Common Grackle (p. 35) lacks a white belly and has a long, thin bill. The male Rose-breasted Grosbeak (p. 49) has a rosy patch on its chest.

Stan's Notes: Named for its distinctive "tow-hee" call (given by both sexes) but known mostly for its other characteristic call, which sounds like "drink-your-tea!" Will hop backward with both feet (bilateral scratching), raking up leaf litter to locate insects and seeds. Male feeds the young most of the time. In southern coastal states, some have red eyes; others have white eyes.

female
p. 137

male

Brown-headed Cowbird

Molothrus ater

SUMMER

Size: 7½" (19 cm)

Male: Glossy black with a chocolate-brown head. Dark eyes. Pointed, sharp gray bill.

Female: dull brown with a pointed, sharp, gray bill

Juvenile: similar to female but with dull-gray plumage and a streaked chest

Nest: no nest; lays eggs in the nests of other birds

Eggs: 5–7; white with brown markings

Incubation: 10–13 days; host birds incubate the eggs

Fledging: 10–11 days; host birds feed the young

Migration: complete, to southern states

Food: insects, seeds; will come to seed feeders

Compare: The male Red-winged Blackbird (p. 31) is slightly larger and has red-and-yellow patches on its upper wings. The Common Grackle (p. 35) has a long tail and lacks the brown head. The European Starling (p. 29) has a shorter tail.

Stan's Notes: Cowbirds are members of the blackbird family. Known as brood parasites, Brown-headed Cowbirds are the only parasitic birds in Maine. Brood parasites lay their eggs in the nests of other birds, leaving the host birds to raise their young. Cowbirds are known to have laid their eggs in the nests of over 200 species of birds. While some birds reject cowbird eggs, most incubate them and raise the young, even to the exclusion of their own. Look for warblers and other birds feeding young birds twice their own size. Named "Cowbird" for its habit of following bison and cattle herds to feed on insects flushed up by the animals.

winter

breeding

European Starling
Sturnus vulgaris

YEAR-ROUND

Size: 7½" (19 cm)

Male: Glittering, iridescent purplish black in spring and summer; duller and speckled with white in fall and winter. Long, pointed, yellow bill in spring; gray in fall. Pointed wings. Short tail.

Female: same as male

Juvenile: similar to adults, with grayish-brown plumage and a streaked chest

Nest: cavity; male and female line the cavity; 2 broods per year

Eggs: 4–6; bluish or greenish without markings

Incubation: 12–14 days; female and male incubate

Fledging: 18–20 days; female and male feed the young

Migration: non-migrator to partial; will move around to find food; some will move to southern states

Food: insects, seeds, fruit; visits seed or suet feeders

Compare: The Common Grackle (p. 35) has a long tail. The male Brown-headed Cowbird (p. 27) has a brown head. Look for the shiny, dark feathers to help identify the European Starling.

Stan's Notes: A great songster, this bird mimics the songs of up to 20 bird species and imitates sounds, including the human voice. Jaws are more powerful when opening than when closing, enabling the bird to pry open crevices to find insects. Often displaces woodpeckers, chickadees, and other cavity-nesting birds. Large families gather with blackbirds in the fall. Not a native bird; 100 starlings were introduced to New York City in 1891 from Europe. Bill changes color with the seasons in spring and fall.

female
p. 149

male

Red-winged Blackbird
Agelaius phoeniceus

SUMMER

Size: 8½" (21.5 cm)

Male: Jet black with red-and-yellow patches (epaulets) on upper wings. Pointed black bill.

Female: heavily streaked brown with a pointed brown bill and white eyebrows

Juvenile: same as female

Nest: cup; female builds; 1–2 broods per year

Eggs: 3–4; bluish green with brown markings

Incubation: 10–12 days; female incubates

Fledging: 11–14 days; female and male feed the young

Migration: complete, to southern states

Food: seeds, insects; visits seed and suet feeders

Compare: The male Brown-headed Cowbird (p. 27) is smaller and glossier and has a brown head. The male Rusty Blackbird is slightly larger (p. 33). The bold red-and-yellow epaulets distinguish the male Red-winged from other blackbirds.

Stan's Notes: One of the most widespread and numerous birds in the state. Found around marshes, wetlands, lakes, and rivers. It is a sure sign of spring when these birds return home. Flocks with as many as 10,000 birds have been reported. Males arrive before the females and sing to defend their territory. The male repeats his call from the top of a cattail while showing off his red-and-yellow shoulder patches. The female chooses a mate and often builds her nest over shallow water in a thick stand of cattails. The male can be aggressive when defending the nest. Red-winged Blackbirds feed mostly on seeds in spring and fall, and on insects throughout the summer.

male

female
p. 236

nonbreeding

Rusty Blackbird
Euphagus carolinus

Size: 9" (22.5 cm)

Male: Glossy black in color with highlights of blue and purple. Bright yellow eyes. Has a short, pointed thin bill. Non-breeding plumage is more of a rusty brown than glossy black.

Female: overall gray bird, feathers have rusty edges, eyes yellow, has a short, pointed thin bill, non-breeding is much browner with a gray rump and black patch around each eye

Juvenile: similar to female

Nest: cup; female builds; 1–2 broods per year

Eggs: 4–5; bluish with brown markings

Incubation: 12–14 days; female incubates

Fledging: 11–13 days; female and male feed the young

Migration: complete, to southeastern states

Food: insects, seeds

Compare: The male Red-winged Blackbird (p. 31) is slightly smaller and has red and yellow markings on shoulders. Smaller than the Common Grackle (p. 35), which has a longer tail.

Stan's Notes: This bird nests across the northern half of Maine in small loose colonies, often preferring more wooded, swampy areas. Male feeds female while she incubates. Gathers in large groups and with other blackbirds to migrate each fall. When in flight, end of tail often appears squared.

Common Grackle
Quiscalus quiscula

YEAR-ROUND
SUMMER

Size: 11–13" (28–33 cm)

Male: Large, iridescent blackbird with bluish-black head and purplish-brown body. Long black tail. Long, thin bill and bright-golden eyes.

Female: similar to male but smaller and duller

Juvenile: similar to female

Nest: cup; female builds; 2 broods per year

Eggs: 4–5; greenish white with brown markings

Incubation: 13–14 days; female incubates

Fledging: 16–20 days; female and male feed the young

Migration: complete, to southern states, non-migrator in part of Maine

Food: fruit, seeds, insects; will come to seed and suet feeders

Compare: The European Starling (p. 29) is much smaller with a speckled appearance and a yellow bill during the breeding season. The male Red-winged Blackbird (p. 31) has bright red-and-yellow shoulder patches (epaulets). The male Rusty Blackbird (p. 33) is smaller and lacks the Grackle's long tail.

Stan's Notes: Usually nests in small colonies of up to 75 pairs but travels with other blackbird species in large flocks. Known to feed in farm fields. The common name is derived from the Latin word *gracula*, meaning "jackdaw," another species of bird and a term that can refer to any bird in the *Quiscalus* genus. The male holds his tail in a deep V shape during flight. The flight pattern is usually level, as opposed to an undulating movement. Unlike most birds, it has larger muscles for opening its mouth than for closing it, enabling it to pry crevices apart to find hidden insects.

in flight

American Crow

Corvus brachyrhynchos

YEAR-ROUND

Size: 18" (45 cm)

Male: All-black bird with black bill, legs, and feet. Can have a purple sheen in direct sunlight.

Female: same as male

Juvenile: same as adults

Nest: platform; female builds; 1 brood per year

Eggs: 4–6; bluish to olive with brown markings

Incubation: 18 days; female incubates

Fledging: 28–35 days; female and male feed the young

Migration: non-migrator to partial migrator; moves around in winter, often into city interiors

Food: fruit, insects, mammals, fish, carrion; comes to seed and suet feeders

Compare: The Common Raven (p. 39) has a larger bill; shaggy throat feathers; a deep, raspy call; and a wedged tail, as seen in flight. Look for the glossy black plumage and squared tail to help identify the American Crow.

Stan's Notes: A familiar bird, found in all habitats. Imitates other birds and human voices. One of the smartest of all birds and very social, often entertaining itself by provoking chases with other birds. Eats roadkill but is rarely hit by vehicles. Can live as long as 15—20 years. Often reuses its nest every year if it's not taken over by a Great Horned Owl. Unmated birds, known as helpers, help to raise the young. Extended families roost together at night, dispersing daily to hunt. Cannot soar on thermals; flaps constantly and glides downward. Gathers in huge communal flocks of up to 10,000 birds in winter.

in flight

Common Raven
Corvus corax

YEAR-ROUND

Size: 22–27" (56–69 cm)

Male: Large all-black bird with a shaggy beard of feathers on the throat and a large black bill. Large wedge-shaped tail, best seen in flight.

Female: same as male

Juvenile: same as adults

Nest: platform; female and male construct; 1 brood per year

Eggs: 4–6; pale green with brown markings

Incubation: 18–21 days; female incubates

Fledging: 38–44 days; female and male feed the young

Migration: non-migrator to partial migrator; moves around to find food in winter

Food: insects, fruit, small animals, carrion

Compare: The American Crow (p. 37) is smaller and lacks the shaggy throat feathers. The Raven glides on flat, outstretched wings, unlike the slight V-shaped wing pattern of the Crow. Listen for the Raven's deep, raspy call to distinguish it from the Crow's higher-pitched call.

Stan's Notes: Considered by some to be the smartest of all birds. Known for its aerial acrobatics and long, swooping dives. Sometimes scavenges with crows and gulls. A cooperative hunter that often communicates the location of a food source to other ravens. Most start to breed at 3–4 years. Complex courtship includes grabbing bills, preening each other and cooing. Long-term pair bond. Uses the same nest site for many years.

soaring

juvenile

drying

Turkey Vulture
Cathartes aura

Size: 26–32" (66–81 cm); up to 6' wingspan

Male: Large and black with a naked red head and legs. In flight, wings are two-toned with a black leading edge and a gray trailing edge. Wing tips end in finger-like projections. Tail is long and squared. Ivory bill.

Female: same as male but slightly smaller

Juvenile: similar to adults, with a gray to blackish head and bill

Nest: no nest or minimal nest, on a cliff or in a cave, sometimes in a hollow tree; 1 brood per year

Eggs: 1–3; white with brown markings

Incubation: 34–41 days; female and male incubate

Fledging: 66–88 days; female and male feed the young

Migration: complete, to southern states, Mexico, and Central and South America

Food: carrion; parents regurgitate to feed the young

Compare: The Bald Eagle (p. 81) is much larger and lacks two-toned wings. Look for the obvious naked red head to identify the Turkey Vulture.

Stan's Notes: The naked head reduces the risk of feather fouling (picking up diseases) from contact with carcasses. It has a strong bill for tearing apart flesh. Unlike hawks and eagles, it has weak feet more suited for walking than grasping. One of the few birds with a developed sense of smell. Mostly mute, making only grunts and groans. Holds its wings in an upright V shape in flight. Teeters from wing tip to wing tip as it soars and hovers. Seen in trees with wings outstretched, sunning itself and drying after a rain.

in flight

juvenile

crests

drying

Double-crested Cormorant

Phalacrocorax auritus

SUMMER
MIGRATION

Size:	31–35" (79–89 cm); up to 4⅓' wingspan
Male:	Large black waterbird with unusual blue eyes and a long, snakelike neck. Large gray bill, with yellow at the base and a hooked tip.
Female:	same as male
Juvenile:	lighter brown with a grayish chest and neck
Nest:	platform; male and female construct; 1 brood per year
Eggs:	3–4; bluish white without markings
Incubation:	25–29 days; female and male incubate
Fledging:	37–42 days; male and female feed the young
Migration:	complete, to southern coastal states, Mexico, and Central America
Food:	small fish, aquatic insects
Compare:	The Turkey Vulture (p. 41) also spreads out its wings to dry in the sun, but it has a naked red head. Look for the long, snakelike neck and large, hooked bill to help identify the Cormorant.

Stan's Notes: Flies in a large V or a line. Usually roosts in large colonies in trees close to water. Swims underwater to catch fish, holding its wings at its sides. This bird's outer feathers soak up water, but its body feathers don't. To dry off, it strikes an upright pose with wings outstretched, facing the sun. Gives grunts, pops, and groans. Named "Double-crested" for the crests on its head, which are not often seen. "Cormorant" is a contraction from *corvus marinus*, meaning "crow" or "raven," and "of the sea."

male

female

Black-and-white Warbler
Mniotilta varia

SUMMER

Size: 5" (13 cm)

Male: Small with zebralike striping and a black-and-white striped crown. Black cheek patch and chin. White belly.

Female: duller than male and lacks a black cheek patch and chin

Juvenile: similar to female

Nest: cup; female builds; 1 brood per year

Eggs: 4–5; white with brown markings

Incubation: 10–11 days; female incubates

Fledging: 9–12 days; female and male feed the young

Migration: complete, to Florida, Mexico, and Central and South America

Food: insects

Compare: Climbs down tree trunks headfirst, like the White-breasted Nuthatch (p. 219) and Red-breasted Nuthatch (p. 215). Look for a small black-and-white bird climbing down trees to identify the Black-and-white Warbler.

Stan's Notes: This is the only warbler species that moves down tree trunks headfirst. Look for it searching for insect eggs in the bark of large trees. Its song sounds like a slowly turning, squeaky wheel going around and around. Female performs a distraction dance to draw predators away from the nest. Constructs its nest on the ground, concealing it under dead leaves or at the base of a tree. Found in a variety of habitats. Common summer resident in the state, although more conspicuous during migration. Most arrive in April and May and leave by September.

male

female

Downy Woodpecker
Dryobates pubescens

YEAR-ROUND

Size: 6" (15 cm)

Male: Small woodpecker with a white belly and black-and-white spotted wings. Red mark on the back of the head and a white stripe down the back. Short black bill.

Female: same as male but lacks the red mark

Juvenile: same as female, some with a red mark near the forehead

Nest: cavity with a round entrance hole; male and female excavate; 1 brood per year

Eggs: 3–5; white without markings

Incubation: 11–12 days; female incubates during the day, male incubates at night

Fledging: 20–25 days; male and female feed the young

Migration: non-migrator

Food: insects, seeds; visits suet and seed feeders

Compare: The Hairy Woodpecker (p. 53) is larger. Look for the Downy's shorter, thinner bill.

Stan's Notes: Abundant and widespread where trees are present. This is perhaps the most common woodpecker in the U.S. Stiff tail feathers help to brace it like a tripod as it clings to a tree. Like other woodpeckers, it has a long, barbed tongue to pull insects from tiny places. Mates drum on branches or hollow logs to announce territory, which is rarely larger than 5 acres (2 ha). Repeats a high-pitched "peek-peek" call. Nest cavity is wider at the bottom than at the top and is lined with fallen wood chips. Male performs most of the brooding. During winter, it will roost in a cavity. Undulates in flight.

female
p. 135

male

Rose-breasted Grosbeak
Pheucticus ludovicianus

SUMMER

Size: 7–8" (18–20 cm)

Male: Plump black-and-white bird with a large triangular, rose-colored patch on the breast. Wing linings are rose red. Large ivory bill.

Female: heavily streaked with obvious white eyebrows and orange-to-yellow wing linings

Juvenile: similar to female

Nest: cup; female and male construct; 1–2 broods per year

Eggs: 3–5; blue-green with brown markings

Incubation: 13–14 days; female and male incubate

Fledging: 9–12 days; female and male feed the young

Migration: complete, to Mexico, Central America, and South America

Food: insects, seeds, fruit; comes to seed feeders

Compare: Male is very distinctive, with no look-alikes. Look for the rose breast patch to identify.

Stan's Notes: Seen in small groups during spring migration. Prefers a mature deciduous forest for nesting. Both sexes sing, but the male sings much louder and clearer. Sings a rich, robin-like song with a chip note in the tune. "Grosbeak" refers to the thick, strong bill, which is used to crush seeds. The rose patch varies in size and shape in each male. Males have white wing patches that flash during flight. Males arrive at the breeding grounds a few days before the females. Several males will come to seed feeders together in spring. When the females arrive, males become territorial and reduce their feeder visits. After fledging, young grosbeaks visit feeders with the adults. Makes short flights from tree to tree with rapid wingbeats.

male

female

Yellow-bellied Sapsucker

Sphyrapicus varius

SUMMER

Size: 8–9" (20–23 cm)

Male: Checkered back with a red forehead, crown and chin. Yellow to tan on the chest and belly. White wing patches are seen flashing in flight.

Female: similar to male but with a white chin

Juvenile: similar to female but dull brown and lacks red markings

Nest: cavity; female and male excavate, often in a live tree; 1 brood per year

Eggs: 5–6; white without markings

Incubation: 12–13 days; female incubates during the day, male incubates at night

Fledging: 25–29 days; female and male feed the young

Migration: complete, to southern states, Mexico, and Central America

Food: insects, tree sap; comes to suet feeders

Compare: The Red-headed Woodpecker (p. 55) has an all-red head. Look for the red chin and crown to identify the male Sapsucker, and the white chin and red crown to identify the female.

Stan's Notes: Found in small woods, forests, and suburban and rural areas. Drills rows of holes in trees to bleed the sap. Oozing sap attracts bugs, which it also eats. Defends its sapping sites from other birds that try to drink from the taps. Does not suck sap; rather, it laps the sticky liquid with its long, bristly tongue. A quiet bird, it makes few vocalizations but will meow like a cat. Drums on hollow branches, but unlike other woodpeckers, its rhythm is irregular. Makes short undulating flights with rapid wingbeats.

male

female

Hairy Woodpecker
Leuconotopicus villosus

YEAR-ROUND

Size: 9" (23 cm)

Male: Black-and-white woodpecker with a white belly. Black wings with rows of white spots. White stripe down the back. Long black bill. Red mark on the back of the head.

Female: same as male but lacks the red mark

Juvenile: grayer version of the female

Nest: cavity with an oval entrance hole; female and male excavate; 1 brood per year

Eggs: 3–6; white without markings

Incubation: 11–15 days; female incubates during the day, male incubates at night

Fledging: 28–30 days; male and female feed the young

Migration: non-migrator, moves around in winter to find food

Food: insects, nuts, seeds; will come to suet and seed feeders

Compare: Much larger than the Downy Woodpecker (p. 47) and has a much longer bill, nearly equal to the width of its head.

Stan's Notes: A common bird in wooded backyards. Announces its arrival with a sharp chirp before landing on feeders. Responsible for eating many destructive forest insects. Uses its barbed tongue to extract insects from trees. Tiny, bristle-like feathers at the base of the bill protect the nostrils from wood dust. Drums on hollow logs, branches, or stovepipes in spring to announce territory. Often prefers to excavate nest cavities in live aspen trees. Excavates a larger, more oval-shaped entrance than the round entrance hole of the Downy Woodpecker. Makes short flights from tree to tree.

juvenile

Red-headed Woodpecker

Melanerpes erythrocephalus

SUMMER

Size: 9" (23 cm)

Male: All-red head with a solid black back. Black wings with large white wing patches seen flashing in flight. Black tail. White chest, belly, and rump. Gray legs and bill.

Female: same as male

Juvenile: grayish-brown head and white chest

Nest: cavity; male excavates with some help from the female; 1 brood per year

Eggs: 4–5; white without markings

Incubation: 12–13 days; female and male incubate

Fledging: 27–30 days; female and male feed the young

Migration: complete; will move to areas with an abundant supply of nuts

Food: insects, nuts, fruit; visits suet and seed feeders

Compare: No other woodpecker in Maine has an all-red head. The Pileated Woodpecker (p. 73) is the only other woodpecker with a solid black back, but it has a partial red head.

Stan's Notes: One of the few non-dimorphic woodpeckers, with males and females that look alike. Bill is strong enough to excavate a nest cavity only in soft, dead trees. Prefers open woodlands or woodland edges with many dead or rotting branches. Nests later than its close relative, the Red-bellied Woodpecker, and will often take its cavity, if vacant. Unlike other woodpeckers, which use nest cavities just once briefly, it may use the same cavity for several years in a row. Often perches on top of dead snags. Stores acorns and other nuts. Gives a shrill, hoarse "churr" call.

male

female

Red-bellied Woodpecker
Melanerpes carolinus

YEAR-ROUND

Size: 9–9½" (23–24 cm)

Male: Black-and-white "zebra-backed" woodpecker with a white rump. Red crown extends down the nape of the neck. Tan chest. Pale-red tinge on the belly, often hard to see.

Female: same as male but with a light-gray crown and a red nape

Juvenile: gray version of adults; lacks a red crown and red nape

Nest: cavity; female and male excavate; 1–2 broods per year

Eggs: 4–5; white without markings

Incubation: 12–14 days; female incubates during the day, male incubates at night

Fledging: 24–27 days; female and male feed the young

Migration: non-migrator; moves around to find food

Food: insects, nuts, fruit; visits suet and seed feeders

Compare: Similar to the Northern Flicker (p. 161) and Yellow-bellied Sapsucker (p. 51). Look for the zebra-striped back to help identify the Red-bellied Woodpecker.

Stan's Notes: Likes shady woodlands, forest edges, and backyards. Digs holes in rotten wood to find spiders, centipedes, beetles, and more. Hammers acorns and berries into crevices of trees for winter food. Returns to the same tree to excavate a new nest below that of the previous year. Often kicked out of nest hole by European Starlings. Undulating flight with rapid wingbeats. Gives a loud "querrr" call and a low "chug-chug-chug." Named for the pale-red tinge on its belly. Expanding its range all over the country.

winter

breeding

Ruddy Turnstone
Arenaria interpres

MIGRATION

Size: 9½" (24 cm)

Male: Breeding male has a white breast and belly with a black bib. Wings and back are black and chestnut. Head has a black-and-white marking. Orange legs. Slightly upturned black bill. Winter male has a brown-and-white head and breast pattern.

Female: similar to male but duller

Juvenile: similar to adults, but black-and-white head has a scaly appearance

Nest: ground; female builds; 1 brood per year

Eggs: 3–4; olive-green with dark markings

Incubation: 22–24 days; male and female incubate

Fledging: 19–21 days; male feeds the young

Migration: complete, to southern coastal states, Mexico, and Central and South America

Food: aquatic insects, fish, mollusks, crustaceans, worms, eggs

Compare: Unusually ornamented shorebird. Look for the striking black-and-white pattern on the head and neck, and orange legs to identify.

Stan's Notes: A common migrant and winter resident. Also known as Rock Plover. Named "Turnstone" because it turns stones over on rocky beaches to find food. Known for its unusual behavior of robbing and eating other birds' eggs. Hangs around crabbing operations to eat scraps from nets. Can be tolerant of humans when feeding. Females often leave before their young leave the nest (fledge), resulting in males raising the young. Males have a bare spot on the belly (brood patch) to warm the young, something only females normally have.

Atlantic Puffin
Fratercula arctica

SUMMER
WINTER

Size: 12" (30 cm)

Male: Black back with white breast and belly. An oversized orange bill with gray base. White face and dark eyes. Orange legs and feet.

Female: same as male

Juvenile: similar to adults, but gray face with a smaller triangular-shaped bill

Nest: cavity; male digs tunnel under a rock, up to 36 inches (90 cm); 1 brood per year

Eggs: 1; white without markings

Incubation: 39–45 days; male and female incubate

Fledging: 38–44 days; male and female feeds the young

Migration: partial; moves out to sea for the winter

Food: fish, aquatic insects

Compare: The unique shape and coloring of this bird and its extremely large bill makes it hard to confuse with any other bird.

Stan's Notes: The Atlantic Puffin is one of the three puffin species in North America. The other two species, Tufted Puffin and Horned Puffin (not shown), are seen on the West coast. Large colony nester, usually on islands. Male will excavate a tunnel up to three times its own length under a rock, ending in a nest chamber. Nest chamber is lined with grass, leaves, and feathers. Adults fly up to 10 miles (16 km) from nest sites and dive down as far as 100 feet (30 m) to catch fish. Young are fed an all-fish diet. Will return to same nest site with same mate each season. Move off land and out to sea in winter. Formerly known as Common Puffin.

female
p. 167

male

Bufflehead
Bucephala albeola

Size: 13–15" (33–38 cm)

Male: A small, striking duck with white sides and a black back. Greenish-purple head, iridescent in bright sun, with a large white head patch.

Female: brownish-gray with a dark brown head and white cheek patch behind the eyes

Juvenile: similar to female

Nest: cavity; female lines old woodpecker cavity; 1 brood per year

Eggs: 8–10; ivory to olive without markings

Incubation: 29–31 days; female incubates

Fledging: 50–55 days; female leads young to food

Migration: complete, along the East coast from Maine to Florida, Mexico, and Central America

Food: aquatic insects

Compare: Male Common Goldeneye (p. 71) is larger, shares the white sides and black back, but lacks the white head patch. Look for the large white bonnet-like patch on a greenish-purple head to help identify the male Bufflehead.

Stan's Notes: A small, common diving duck, almost always seen in small groups or with other duck species on rivers, ponds, lakes, and along the coast. Most commonly found in sheltered bays and coastal harbors. Winters in the southern half of Maine. Nests in vacant woodpecker holes. When cavities in trees are scarce, known to use a burrow in an earthen bank or will use a nest box. Lines the cavity with fluffy down feathers. Unlike other ducks, the young stay in the nest for up to two days before they venture out with their mothers. The female is very territorial and remains with the same mate for many years.

female p. 179

male

Lesser Scaup
Aythya affinis

MIGRATION

Size: 16–17" (40–43 cm)

Male: Appears mostly black with bold white sides and a gray back. Chest and head look nearly black, but head appears purple with green highlights in direct sun. Bright-yellow eyes.

Female: overall brown with a dull-white patch at the base of a light-gray bill; yellow eyes

Juvenile: same as female

Nest: ground; female builds; 1 brood per year

Eggs: 8–14; olive-buff without markings

Incubation: 22–28 days; female incubates

Fledging: 45–50 days; female teaches the young to feed

Migration: complete, to southern states, Mexico, Central America, and northern South America; moves around to find open water in winter

Food: aquatic plants and insects

Compare: The male Ring-necked Duck (p. 67) has a bold white ring around its bill and a black back, compared with male Lesser Scaup's gray back. Male Ring-necked lacks the bold white sides of the male Lesser Scaup.

Stan's Notes: A common migrating diving duck in Maine. Often in large flocks on lakes, ponds, and sewage lagoons during migration. Submerges completely to feed on the bottom (unlike dabbling ducks, which tip forward to reach the bottom). Note the bold white stripe under the wings when in flight. The male leaves the female when she starts incubating eggs. Has an interesting babysitting arrangement: groups of young (crèches) are tended by one to three adult females. Prefers fresh water, but can be seen along the coast. Doesn't breed in Maine.

female
p. 185

male

Ring-necked Duck
Aythya collaris

SUMMER

Size: 16–19" (41–48 cm)

Male: Striking black duck with light-gray-to-white sides. Blue bill with a bold white ring and a thinner ring at the base. Peaked head with a sloped forehead.

Female: brown with darker-brown back and crown, light-brown sides, gray face, white line behind eyes, white eye-ring, white ring around the bill, and peaked head

Juvenile: similar to female

Nest: ground; female builds; 1 brood per year

Eggs: 8–10; olive-gray to brown without markings

Incubation: 26–27 days; female incubates

Fledging: 49–56 days; female teaches the young to feed

Migration: complete, to southern states, West Indies, Mexico, and Central America

Food: aquatic plants and insects

Compare: Male Lesser Scaup (p. 65) is similar in size, but it has a gray back, unlike the black back of the male Ring-necked Duck. Look for the blue bill with a bold white ring to identify the male Ring-necked Duck.

Stan's Notes: A common breeding duck in Maine. Usually in larger freshwater lakes rather than saltwater marshes, in small flocks or pairs. Watch for this duck to dive underwater to forage. Springs up off the water to take flight. Flattens its crown when diving. Male gives a quick series of grating barks and grunts. Female gives high-pitched peeps. Named "Ring-necked" for its cinnamon collar, which is difficult to see in the field.

male

female
p. 189

Hooded Merganser
Lophodytes cucullatus

YEAR-ROUND
SUMMER

Size: 16–19" (41–48 cm)

Male: Black and white with rust-brown sides. Crest "hood" raises to show a large white patch on each side of the head. Long, thin black bill.

Female: brown and rust with ragged, rust-red "hair" and a long, thin brown bill

Juvenile: similar to female

Nest: cavity; female lines an old woodpecker cavity or a nest box near water; 1 brood per year

Eggs: 10–12; white without markings

Incubation: 32–33 days; female incubates

Fledging: 71 days; female feeds the young

Migration: complete, to coastal states and Mexico

Food: small fish, aquatic insects, crustaceans

Compare: The male Bufflehead (p. 63) is smaller and has white sides. The male Wood Duck (p. 267) has a green head. The male Common Merganser (p. 273) is much larger. The white patch on the head and rust-brown sides distinguish the male Hoodie.

Stan's Notes: A small diving duck, found in shallow ponds, sloughs, lakes, and rivers, usually in small groups. It is a summer breeding duck in Maine, rarely seen away from wooded areas, where it nests in natural cavities or nest boxes. Quick, low flight across the water, with fast wingbeats. Male has a deep, rolling call. Female gives a hoarse quack. Nests in wooded areas. Female will lay some eggs in the nests of other mergansers, goldeneyes, or Wood Ducks (egg dumping), resulting in 20–25 eggs in some nests. Rarely, she shares a nest, sitting with a Wood Duck. Not as common as the Common Merganser.

female
p. 193

male

Common Goldeneye
Bucephala clangula

Size: 18–20" (45–51 cm)

Male: Mostly white duck with a black back and a large, puffy green head. Large white spot on the face. Bright-golden eyes. Dark bill.

Female: large dark-brown head with a gray body and a white collar, bright-golden eyes, yellow-tipped, dark bill

Juvenile: same as female but has dark eyes

Nest: cavity; female lines an old woodpecker cavity; 1 brood per year

Eggs: 8–10; light green without markings

Incubation: 28–32 days; female incubates

Fledging: 56–59 days; female leads the young to food

Migration: partial to non-migrator in Maine

Food: aquatic plants, insects, fish, mollusks

Compare: Similar to the black-and-white male Lesser Scaup (p. 65), which is smaller. Look for the distinctive white spot on the sides of the face and the golden eyes to identify the male Common Goldeneye.

Stan's Notes: Known for the loud whistling sound produced by its wings during flight. During late winter and early spring, the male performs elaborate mating displays that include throwing his head back and calling a raspy note. The female will lay some of her eggs in other goldeneye nests or in the nests of other species (called egg dumping), causing some mothers to incubate as many as 30 eggs in a brood. Named for its bright-golden eyes. Moves to southern and coastal Maine during winter.

male

female

Pileated Woodpecker
Dryocopus pileatus

YEAR-ROUND

Size: 19" (48 cm)

Male: Crow-size woodpecker with a black back and bright-red forehead, crest, and mustache. Long gray bill. White leading edge of wings flashes brightly during flight.

Female: same as male but with a black forehead; lacks a red mustache

Juvenile: similar to adults but duller and browner

Nest: cavity; male and female excavate; 1 brood per year

Eggs: 3–5; white without markings

Incubation: 15–18 days; female incubates during the day, male incubates at night

Fledging: 26–28 days; female and male feed the young

Migration: non-migrator; moves around to find food

Food: insects; will come to suet and peanut feeders

Compare: The Red-headed Woodpecker (p. 55) is about half the size and has an all-red head. Look for the bright-red crest and exceptionally large size to identify the Pileated Woodpecker.

Stan's Notes: Our largest woodpecker. The common name comes from the Latin *pileatus*, which means "wearing a cap." A relatively shy bird that prefers large tracts of woodland. Drums on hollow branches, stovepipes, and so forth to announce its territory. Excavates oval holes up to several feet long in tree trunks, looking for insects to eat. Large wood chips lie on the ground by excavated trees. Favorite food is carpenter ants. Feeds regurgitated insects to its young. Young emerge from the nest looking just like the adults.

soaring

Osprey
Pandion haliaetus

SUMMER

Size: 21–24" (53–61 cm); up to 5½' wingspan

Male: Large eagle-like bird with a white chest, belly, and head. Dark eye line. Nearly black back. Black "wrist" marks on the wings. Dark bill.

Female: same as male but slightly larger and with a necklace of brown streaks

Juvenile: similar to adults, with a light-tan breast

Nest: platform on a raised wooden platform, man-made tower or tall dead tree; female and male build; 1 brood per year

Eggs: 2–4; white with brown markings

Incubation: 32–42 days; female and male incubate

Fledging: 48–58 days; male and female feed the young

Migration: complete, to southern coastal states, Mexico, and Central and South America

Food: fish

Compare: The juvenile Bald Eagle (p. 81) is brown with white speckles. The adult Bald Eagle has an all-white head and tail. Look for the white belly and dark eye line to identify the Osprey.

Stan's Notes: The only species in its family, and the only raptor that plunges into water feetfirst to catch fish. Always near water. Can hover for a few seconds before diving. Carries fish in a head-first position for better aerodynamics. Wings angle back in flight. Often harassed by Bald Eagles for its catch. Gives a high-pitched, whistle-like call, often calling in flight as a warning. Mates have a long-term pair bond. Northern birds may not migrate to the same wintering ground. Was nearly extinct but is now doing well.

in flight

Black-crowned Night-Heron
Nycticorax nycticorax

Size: 22–27" (56–69 cm); up to 3½' wingspan

Male: A stocky, hunched and inactive heron with black back and crown, white belly, and gray wings. Long dark bill and bright-red eyes. Short dull-yellow legs. Breeding adult has 2 long white plumes on crown.

Female: same as male

Juvenile: golden-brown head and back with white spots; streaked breast; yellow-orange eyes and brown bill

Nest: platform; female and male build; 1 brood per year

Eggs: 3–5; light blue without markings

Incubation: 24–26 days; female and male incubate

Fledging: 42–48 days; female and male feed the young

Migration: complete, to southern coastal states, Mexico and Central America

Food: fish, aquatic insects

Compare: A perching Great Blue Heron (p. 263) looks twice the size of a Black-crowned. Look for a short-necked heron with a black back and crown.

Stan's Notes: A very secretive bird, this heron is most active near dawn and dusk (crepuscular). It hunts alone, but it nests in small colonies. Roosts in trees during the day. Often squawks if disturbed from the daytime roost. Often seen being harassed by other herons during the day. Stalks quiet backwaters in search of small fish and crabs.

breeding

winter

Common Loon
Gavia immer

Size: 28–36" (71–91 cm)

Male: Checkerboard back, black head, white necklace. Deep-red eyes. Long, pointed black bill. Winter plumage has a gray body and bill.

Female: same as male

Juvenile: similar to winter plumage but lacks red eyes

Nest: ground, usually at the shoreline; female and male build; 1 brood per year

Eggs: 2; olive-brown; occasionally brown markings

Incubation: 26–31 days; female and male incubate

Fledging: 75–80 days; female and male feed the young

Migration: complete, to southern states, East and Gulf Coast and Mexico

Food: fish, aquatic insects, crayfish, salamanders

Compare: The Double-crested Cormorant (p. 43) has a black chest and gray bill with a hooked tip and yellow at the base. Look for the checkerboard back to identify the Common Loon.

Stan's Notes: A wonderful bird that represents the wilderness of the lakes of Maine. Nests across inland Maine, moving to the coast in the winter. Hunts for fish by sight; prefers clear, clean lakes. A great swimmer, but its legs are set so far back that it has a hard time walking. "Loon" comes from the Scandinavian *lom*, meaning "lame," for the awkward way it walks. To take off, it faces into the wind and runs on the water while flapping. Its wailing call suggests wild laughter, which led to the phrase "crazy as a loon." Also gives soft hoots. In the water, young ride on their parents' backs for about 10 days. Adults perform distraction displays to protect the young. Very sensitive to disturbance during nesting and will abandon the nest.

soaring

juvenile

soaring
juvenile

Bald Eagle
Haliaeetus leucocephalus

YEAR-ROUND

Size: 31–37" (79–94 cm); up to 7½' wingspan

Male: White head and tail contrast sharply with the dark-brown to black body and wings. Large, curved yellow bill and yellow feet.

Female: same as male but larger

Juvenile: dark brown with white speckles and spots on the body and wings; gray bill

Nest: massive platform, usually in a tree; female and male build; 1 brood per year

Eggs: 2–3; off-white without markings

Incubation: 34–36 days; female and male incubate

Fledging: 75–90 days; female and male feed the young

Migration: non-migrator to partial, to coastal states

Food: fish, carrion, birds (mainly ducks)

Compare: The Turkey Vulture (p. 41) is smaller, has two-toned wings and holds them in a V shape in flight. The Eagle holds its wings straight out.

Stan's Notes: Nearly became extinct due to DDT poisoning and illegal killing. Now making a comeback in North America. Returns to the same nest each year, adding more sticks and enlarging it to huge proportions, at times up to 1,000 pounds (450 kg). In their midair mating ritual, one eagle flips upside down and locks talons with another. Both tumble, then break apart to continue flight. Not uncommon for juveniles to perform this mating ritual even though they have not reached breeding age. Long-term pair bond but will switch mates when not successful at reproducing. Juveniles attain the white head and tail at 4–5 years of age.

female
p. 113

male

Indigo Bunting
Passerina cyanea

SUMMER

Size: 5½" (14 cm)

Male: Vibrant-blue finch-like bird. Dark markings scattered on wings and tail.

Female: light-brown with faint markings

Juvenile: similar to female

Nest: cup; female builds; 2 broods per year

Eggs: 3–4; pale blue or sometimes white without markings

Incubation: 12–13 days; female incubates

Fledging: 10–11 days; female feeds the young

Migration: complete, to southern Florida, Mexico, and Central and South America

Food: insects, seeds, fruit; will visit seed feeders

Compare: The male Eastern Bluebird (p. 89) is larger and has a rust-red chest. Look for the bright-blue plumage to identify the male Indigo Bunting.

Stan's Notes: Seen along woodland edges and in parks and yards, feeding on insects. Comes to seed feeders early in spring, before insects are plentiful. Usually only the males are noticed. The male often sings from treetops to attract a mate. The female is quiet. Actually a gray bird, without blue pigment in its feathers: like Blue Jays and other blue birds, sunlight is refracted within the structure of the feathers, making them appear blue. Plumage is iridescent in direct sun, duller in shade. Molts in spring to acquire body feathers with gray tips, which quickly wear off, revealing the bright-blue plumage. Molts in fall and appears like the female during winter. Migrates at night in flocks of 5–10 birds. Males return before the females and juveniles, often to the nest site of the preceding year. Juveniles move to within a mile of their birth site.

Tree Swallow
Tachycineta bicolor

SUMMER

Size: 5–6" (13–15 cm)

Male: Blue-green in spring, greener in fall. Changes color in direct sunlight. White from chin to belly. Long, pointed wing tips. Notched tail.

Female: similar to male but duller

Juvenile: grayish brown with a white belly and a grayish breast band

Nest: cavity; female and male line a vacant wood-pecker cavity or nest box; 2 broods per year

Eggs: 4–6; white without markings

Incubation: 13–16 days; female incubates

Fledging: 20–24 days; female and male feed the young

Migration: complete, to southern coastal states, Mexico, and Central America

Food: insects

Compare: The Purple Martin (p. 91) is much larger and darker. The Barn Swallow (p. 87) has a rusty belly and a long, deeply forked tail. Look for the white chin, chest, and belly and the notched tail to help identify the Tree Swallow.

Stan's Notes: First swallow species to return each spring. Found at coastal beaches, freshwater ponds, lakes, rivers, and farm fields. Often seen flying back and forth across fields, feeding on insects. Can be attracted to your yard with a nest box. Competes with the Eastern Bluebird for tree cavities and nest boxes. Builds a grass nest within and will travel long distances, looking for dropped feathers for the lining. Watch for it playing and chasing after feathers. Gives a series of gurgles and chirps. Chatters when upset or threatened. Eats many nuisance bugs. Families gather in large flocks for migration.

85

Barn Swallow
Hirundo rustica

SUMMER

Size:	7" (18 cm)
Male:	Sleek swallow. Blue-black back, cinnamon belly, and reddish-brown chin. White spots on a long, deeply forked tail.
Female:	same as male but with a whitish belly
Juvenile:	similar to adults, with a tan belly and chin and a shorter tail
Nest:	cup; female and male build; 2 broods per year
Eggs:	4–5; white with brown markings
Incubation:	13–17 days; female incubates
Fledging:	18–23 days; female and male feed the young
Migration:	complete, to South America
Food:	insects (prefers beetles, wasps, flies)
Compare:	The Tree Swallow (p. 85) is white from chin to belly. The Purple Martin (p. 91) is larger and has a dark-purple belly. The Chimney Swift (p. 101) has a narrow, pointed tail. Look for the deeply forked tail to identify the Barn Swallow.

Stan's Notes: Seen in wetlands, farms, suburban yards, and parks. Maine has six swallow species, but this is the only one with a deeply forked tail. Unlike other swallows, it rarely glides in flight. Usually flies low over land or water. Drinks as it flies, skimming water, or will sip water droplets on wet leaves. Bathes while flying through rain or sprinklers. Gives a twittering warble, followed by a mechanical sound. Builds a mud nest with up to 1,000 beak-loads of mud. Nests on barns and houses, under bridges, and in other sheltered places. Often nests in colonies of 4–6 birds; sometimes nests alone.

Eastern Bluebird

Sialia sialis

**YEAR-ROUND
SUMMER**

Size: 7" (18 cm)

Male: Sky-blue head, back, and tail. Rust-red breast and white belly.

Female: grayer than male, with a faint rusty breast and faint blue wings and tail

Juvenile: similar to female but with spots on the breast and blue wing markings

Nest: cavity, vacant woodpecker cavity or nest box; female adds a soft lining; 2 broods per year

Eggs: 4–5; pale blue without markings

Incubation: 12–14 days; female incubates

Fledging: 15–18 days; male and female feed the young

Migration: complete to non-migrator, to southern states

Food: insects, fruit; comes to shallow dishes with live or dead mealworms, and to suet feeders

Compare: The male Indigo Bunting (p. 83) is nearly all blue. The Blue Jay (p. 93) is much larger and has a crest. Look for the rusty breast to help identify the Eastern Bluebird.

Stan's Notes: A summer resident of open fields and agricultural areas. Nearly eliminated from Maine due to a lack of nest cavities. Thanks to people who installed thousands of nestboxes, bluebirds now thrive. Prefers open habitats, such as farm fields, pastures, and roadsides, but also likes forest edges, parks, and yards. Easily tamed. Often perches on trees or fence posts and drops to the ground to grab bugs, especially grasshoppers. Makes short flights from tree to tree. Song is a distinctive "churlee chur churlee." The rust-red breast is like that of the American Robin, its cousin. The young of the first brood help raise the second brood.

male

female

Purple Martin
Progne subis

SUMMER

Size: 7½" (21.5 cm)

Male: Iridescent with a purple-to-black head, back, and belly. Black wings and a notched black tail.

Female: grayish-purple head and back, darker wings and tail, whitish belly

Juvenile: same as female

Nest: cavity; female and male line the cavity of the house; 1 brood per year

Eggs: 4–5; white without markings

Incubation: 15–18 days; female incubates

Fledging: 26–30 days; male and female feed the young

Migration: complete, to South America

Food: insects

Compare: Usually seen only in groups. The male Purple Martin is the only swallow with a very dark-purplish belly.

Stan's Notes: The largest swallow species in North America. Once nested in tree cavities; now nests almost exclusively in man-made, apartment-style houses. The most successful colonies often nest in multiunit nest boxes within 100 feet (30 m) of a human dwelling near a lake. Main diet consists of dragonflies, not mosquitoes, as once thought. Gives a continuous stream of chirps, creaks, and rattles, along with a shout-like "churrr" and chortle. Often drinks in flight, skimming water, and bathes in flight, flying through rain. Returns to the same nest site each year; the males arrive before the females and yearlings. The young leave to form new colonies. Large colonies gather in fall before migrating to South America.

YEAR-ROUND

Blue Jay
Cyanocitta cristata

Size: 12" (30 cm)

Male: Bright light-blue-and-white bird with a black necklace and gray belly. Large crest moves up and down at will. White face, wing bars, and tip of tail. Black tail bands.

Female: same as male

Juvenile: same as adult but duller

Nest: cup; female and male construct; 1–2 broods per year

Eggs: 4–5; green to blue with brown markings

Incubation: 16–18 days; female incubates

Fledging: 17–21 days; female and male feed the young

Migration: non-migrator to partial; will move around in winter to find an abundant food source

Food: insects, fruit, carrion, seeds, nuts; visits seed feeders, ground feeders with corn or peanuts

Compare: The Belted Kingfisher (p. 95) has a larger, more ragged crest. The Eastern Bluebird (p. 89) is much smaller and has a rust-red breast. Look for the large crest to help identify the Blue Jay.

Stan's Notes: Highly intelligent, solving problems, gathering food, and communicating more than other birds. Loud and noisy; mimics other birds. Known as the alarm of the forest, screaming at intruders. Imitates hawk calls around feeders to scare off other birds. One of the few birds to cache food; can remember where it hid thousands of nuts. Carries food in a pouch under its tongue (sublingually). Eats eggs and young birds from other nests. Feathers lack blue pigment; refracted sunlight causes the blue appearance.

male

female

Belted Kingfisher
Megaceryle alcyon

YEAR-ROUND
SUMMER

Size: 12–14" (30–36 cm)

Male: Blue with white belly, blue-gray chest band, and black wing tips. Ragged crest moves up and down at will. Large head. Long, thick, black bill. White spot by eyes. Red-brown eyes.

Female: same as male but with rusty flanks and a rusty chest band below the blue-gray band

Juvenile: similar to female

Nest: cavity; female and male excavate in a bank of a river, lake or cliff; 1 brood per year

Eggs: 6–7; white without markings

Incubation: 23–24 days; female and male incubate

Fledging: 23–24 days; female and male feed the young

Migration: complete, to southern states, Mexico, and Central and South America; winters in coastal Maine

Food: small fish

Compare: The Blue Jay (p. 93) is lighter blue and has a plain gray chest and belly. The Belted Kingfisher is rarely found away from water.

Stan's Notes: Usually found at the bank of a river, lake, or large stream. Perches on a branch near water, dives in headfirst to catch a small fish, then returns to the branch to feed. Parents drop dead fish into the water to teach their young to dive. Can't pass bones through its digestive tract; regurgitates bone pellets after meals. Gives a loud call that sounds like a machine gun. Mates know each other by their calls. Digs a tunnel up to 4 feet (1 m) long to a nest chamber. Small white patches on dark wing tips flash during flight.

Chestnut-sided Warbler
Setophaga pensylvanica

SUMMER

Size: 5" (13 cm)

Male: Colorful combination of a bright-yellow cap, black mask, and white face, with a white chest and belly. Chestnut flanks. Gray wings with 2 yellow wing bars. White undertail.

Female: similar to male, with duller brown flanks

Juvenile: similar to female, with a lime-green head and back, white eye-ring and bright-yellow wing bars; lacks chestnut sides

Nest: cup; female builds; 1 brood per year

Eggs: 3–5; white with brown markings

Incubation: 12–13 days; female incubates

Fledging: 10–12 days; female and male feed the young

Migration: complete, to Central America

Food: insects, berries

Compare: The Yellow-rumped Warbler (p. 221) has yellow patches on its sides and rump. The Yellow Warbler (p. 313) is nearly all yellow. Look for the yellow cap and chestnut flanks to help identify the Chestnut-sided Warbler.

Stan's Notes: A very attractive warbler, named for the chestnut patches on its sides. Prefers an open, young aspen forest. During migration, it is often attracted to backyard water gardens that have a small trickling stream. Look for it in spring, hopping high up in trees while it hunts for insects. Usually you will get only a glimpse of this fast-moving bird. Holds tail in an uplifted position, showing the white undertail. It is not uncommon for it to approach people near its nest in defense of the site.

Brown Creeper
Certhia americana

YEAR-ROUND

Size: 5" (13 cm)

Male: Small, thin, nearly camouflaged brown bird. White from chin to belly. White eyebrows. Dark eyes and a thin, curved bill. Tail is long and stiff.

Female: same as male

Juvenile: same as adults

Nest: cup; female constructs; 1 brood per year

Eggs: 5–6; white with tiny brown markings

Incubation: 14–17 days; female incubates; male feeds the female during incubation

Fledging: 13–16 days; female and male feed the young

Migration: partial to non-migrator; moves around to find food in winter

Food: insects, nuts, seeds

Compare: The Red-breasted Nuthatch (p. 215) and White-breasted Nuthatch (p. 219) climb down tree trunks, not up. To spot a Brown Creeper, look for a small brown bird with a white belly creeping up trees.

Stan's Notes: A forest bird, commonly found in wooded habitats. Will fly from the top of one tree trunk to the bottom of another, then work its way to the top, looking for caterpillars, spider eggs, and more. Its long tail has tiny spines underneath, which help it cling to trees. Uses its camouflage coloring to hide in plain sight: it spreads out flat on a branch or trunk and won't move. Often builds its nest behind the loose bark of a dead or dying tree. Young follow their parents around, creeping up trees soon after fledging.

Chimney Swift
Chaetura pelagica

SUMMER

Size: 5" (13 cm)

Male: Nondescript, cigar-shaped bird, usually seen in flight. Long, thin, brown body. Pointed tail and head. Long, backswept wings, longer than the body.

Female: same as male

Juvenile: same as adults

Nest: half cup; female and male construct; 1 brood per year

Eggs: 4–5; white without markings

Incubation: 19–21 days; female and male incubate

Fledging: 28–30 days; female and male feed the young

Migration: complete, to South America

Food: insects caught in midair

Compare: The Purple Martin (p. 91) is much larger and darker. The Barn Swallow (p. 87) has a deeply forked tail. Tree Swallows (p. 85) have a white belly and blue-green back. Look for the cigar shape to identify the Chimney Swift in flight.

Stan's Notes: One of the fastest fliers in the bird world. Spends all day flying, rarely perching. Flies in groups, feeding on insects flying 100 feet (30 m) or higher up in the air. Often called a Flying Cigar due to its body shape, which is pointed at both ends. Drinks and bathes during flight, skimming water. Gives a unique in-flight twittering call, often heard before the bird is seen. Hundreds roost in large chimneys, giving it the common name. Builds its nest with tiny twigs, cementing it with saliva and attaching it to the inside of a chimney or a hollow tree. Usually only one nest per chimney.

Chipping Sparrow
Spizella passerina

SUMMER

Size: 5" (13 cm)

Male: Small gray-brown sparrow with clear-gray chest, white eyebrows, thin black eye line and rusty crown. Thin gray-black bill. 2 faint wing bars.

Female: same as male

Juvenile: similar to adults, with streaking on the chest; lacks a rusty crown

Nest: cup; female builds; 2 broods per year

Eggs: 3–5; blue-green with brown markings

Incubation: 11–14 days; female incubates

Fledging: 10–12 days; female and male feed the young

Migration: complete, to southern states, Mexico, and Central America

Food: insects, seeds; will come to ground feeders

Compare: The Song Sparrow (p. 117) and female House Finch (p. 109) have heavily streaked chests. The rusty crown and black eye line help identify the Chipping Sparrow.

Stan's Notes: A common garden or yard bird, often seen feeding on dropped seeds beneath feeders. Gathers in large family groups to feed in preparation for migration. Migrates at night in flocks of 20–30 birds. The common name comes from the male's fast "chip" call. Often just called a Chippy. Builds nest low in dense shrubs and almost always lines it with animal hair. Comfortable with people, allowing you to approach closely before it flies away.

Common Redpoll
Acanthis flammea

WINTER

Size: 5" (13 cm)

Male: Sparrow-like bird with a bright-red crown and raspberry red on the chest. Black spot on the chin. Heavily streaked back.

Female: similar to male but lacks red on the chest

Juvenile: browner than adults, with dark streaking on the chest; lacks a red crown

Nest: cup; female builds; 1 brood (occasionally 2) per year

Eggs: 4–5; pale green with purple markings

Incubation: 10–11 days; female incubates

Fledging: 11–12 days; female and male feed the young

Migration: irruptive; moves from Canada into Maine in some winters

Food: seeds, insects; will come to seed feeders

Compare: Male Purple Finch (p. 281) is slightly larger and has a red back and rump. Male House Finch (p. 279) is similar, but it has an orange-red rump. Look for the bright-red crown and black spot under the bill to identify the male Common Redpoll.

Stan's Notes: This bird winters in the state after summering in the far reaches of Canada. Moves from location to location, wheeling around in the sky before landing at feeders. Visits feeders in small to large flocks. Flocks of up 100 birds are not uncommon but are not seen at all in some winters. Bathes in open water or snow in winter. Like the Black-capped Chickadee, it can be tamed and fed by hand. Gives a zipping call in long strings that last 30 seconds or more. Also gives a nasal, rising whistle.

Pine Siskin
Spinus pinus

YEAR-ROUND

Size: 5" (13 cm)

Male: Small brown finch with heavy streaking on the back, breast, and belly. Yellow wing bars. Yellow at the base of the tail. Thin bill.

Female: similar to male, with less yellow

Juvenile: similar to adult, with a light-yellow tinge over the breast and chin

Nest: cup; female builds; 2 broods

Eggs: 3–4; greenish blue with brown markings

Incubation: 12–13 days; female incubates

Fledging: 14–15 days; female and male feed the young

Migration: non-migrator to irruptive; moves around the U.S. in search of food

Food: seeds, insects; will come to seed feeders

Compare: The female Purple Finch (p. 121) has white eyebrows. The female House Finch (p. 109) lacks yellow. The female American Goldfinch (p. 305) has white wing bars. Look for the yellow wing bars to identify the Pine Siskin.

Stan's Notes: Usually considered a winter finch. It is a year-round breeding resident of Maine. It can be more inconspicuous in some years, and absent in some areas in other years. Seen in flocks of up to 20 birds, often with other finch species. Will come to thistle feeders. Gives a series of high-pitched, wheezy calls. Also gives a wheezing twitter. Breeds in small groups. Builds nest toward the end of coniferous branches, where needles are dense, helping to conceal. Nests are often only a few feet apart. Male feeds the female during incubation. Juveniles lose the yellow tint by late summer of their first year.

male
p. 279

female

House Finch

Haemorhous mexicanus

YEAR-ROUND

Size: 5" (13 cm)

Female: Plain brown with heavy streaking on a white chest.

Male: red-to-orange face, throat, chest, and rump, brown cap, brown marking behind the eyes, streaked belly and wings

Juvenile: similar to female

Nest: cup, occasionally in a cavity; female builds; 2 broods per year

Eggs: 4–5; pale blue, lightly marked

Incubation: 12–14 days; female incubates

Fledging: 15–19 days; female and male feed the young

Migration: non-migrator to partial migrator; will move around to find food

Food: seeds, fruit, leaf buds; visits seed feeders and feeders that offer grape jelly

Compare: The female Purple Finch (p. 121) has bold white eyebrows. The Pine Siskin (p. 107) has yellow wing bars and a smaller bill. The female American Goldfinch (p. 305) has a clear chest. Look for the heavily streaked chest to help identify the female House Finch.

Stan's Notes: Can be a common bird at your feeders. A very social bird, visiting feeders in small flocks. Likes to nest in hanging flower baskets. Male sings a loud, cheerful warbling song. Incubating female is fed by the male. It was originally introduced to Long Island, New York, from the western U.S. in the 1940s. Now found throughout the country. Suffers from a disease that causes the eyes to crust, resulting in blindness and death.

House Wren
Troglodytes aedon

SUMMER

Size: 5" (13 cm)

Male: All-brown bird with lighter-brown markings on the wings and tail. Slightly curved brown bill. Often holds tail upward.

Female: same as male

Juvenile: same as adults

Nest: cavity; female and male line just about any nest cavity; 2 broods per year

Eggs: 4–6; tan with brown markings

Incubation: 10–13 days; female and male incubate

Fledging: 12–15 days; female and male feed the young

Migration: complete, to southern states and Mexico

Food: insects, spiders, snails

Compare: Look for House Wren's long curved bill and long upturned tail to differentiate it from sparrows. All other species of wrens have eyebrows.

Stan's Notes: A prolific songster. During the mating season, sings from dawn to dusk. Seen in brushy yards, parks, woodlands, and along forest edges. Easily attracted to a nest box. In spring, the male chooses several prospective nesting cavities and places a few small twigs in each. The female inspects all of them and finishes constructing the nest in the cavity of her choice. She fills the cavity with short twigs and then lines a small depression at the back with pine needles and grass. She often has trouble fitting longer twigs through the entrance hole and tries many different directions and approaches until she is successful.

female

male
p. 83

Indigo Bunting
Passerina cyanea

SUMMER

Size: 5½" (14 cm)

Female: Light-brown, finch-like bird. Faint streaking on a light-tan chest. Wings have a very faint blue cast and indistinct wing bars.

Male: vibrant blue with scattered dark markings on wings and tail

Juvenile: similar to female

Nest: cup; female builds; 2 broods per year

Eggs: 3–4; pale blue or sometimes white without markings

Incubation: 12–13 days; female incubates

Fledging: 10–11 days; female feeds the young

Migration: complete, to southern Florida, Mexico, and Central and South America

Food: insects, seeds, fruit; will visit seed feeders

Compare: The female Purple Finch (p. 121) has white eyebrows and heavy streaking on the chest. The female House Finch (p. 109) has a heavily streaked chest. The female American Goldfinch (p. 305) has white wing bars. Look for the faint blue cast on the wings to help identify the female Indigo Bunting.

Stan's Notes: Seen along woodland edges and in parks and yards, feeding on insects. Comes to seed feeders early in spring, before insects are plentiful. Secretive, plain, and quiet; usually only the males are noticed. The male often sings from treetops to attract a mate. Migrates at night in flocks of 5–10 birds. Males return before the females and juveniles, often to the nest site of the preceding year. Juveniles move to within a mile of their birth site.

male
p. 223

female

Dark-eyed Junco
Junco hyemalis

YEAR-ROUND

Size: 5½" (14 cm)

Female: Plump, dark-eyed bird with a tan-to-brown chest, head and back. White belly. Ivory-to-pink bill. White outer tail feathers appear like a white V in flight.

Male: round with gray plumage

Juvenile: similar to female, with streaking on the breast and head

Nest: cup; female and male build; 2 broods per year

Eggs: 3–5; white with reddish-brown markings

Incubation: 12–13 days; female incubates

Fledging: 10–13 days; male and female feed the young

Migration: complete, across the U.S.; non-migrator in Maine

Food: seeds, insects; visits ground and seed feeders

Compare: Rarely confused with any other bird. Look for the ivory-to-pink bill and small flocks feeding under feeders to help identify the female Dark-eyed Junco.

Stan's Notes: One of the most common winter birds in the state. Migrates from Canada to Maine and areas farther south. Stays in the state year-round. Females tend to migrate farther south than males. Adheres to a rigid social hierarchy, with dominant birds chasing the less dominant ones. Look for the white outer tail feathers flashing in flight. Often seen in small flocks on the ground, where it uses its feet to simultaneously "double-scratch" to expose seeds and insects. Eats many weed seeds. Nests in a wide variety of wooded habitats. Several subspecies of Dark-eyed Junco were previously considered to be separate species.

Song Sparrow
Melospiza melodia

YEAR-ROUND
SUMMER

Size: 5–6" (13–15 cm)

Male: Common brown sparrow with heavy dark streaks on the chest coalescing into a central dark spot.

Female: same as male

Juvenile: similar to adults, with a finely streaked chest; lacks a central dark spot

Nest: cup; female builds; 2 broods per year

Eggs: 3–6; blue to green, with red-brown markings

Incubation: 12–14 days; female incubates

Fledging: 9–12 days; female and male feed the young

Migration: complete, to southern states; non-migrator in southern Maine

Food: insects, seeds; only rarely comes to ground feeders with seeds

Compare: Similar to other brown sparrows. Look for the heavily streaked chest with a central dark spot to help identify the Song Sparrow.

Stan's Notes: There are many subspecies of this bird, but the dark spot in the center of the chest appears in every variety. A constant songster, repeating its loud, clear song every few minutes. The song varies from region to region but has the same basic structure. Sings from thick shrubs to defend a small territory, beginning with three notes and finishing up with a trill. A ground feeder, it will "double-scratch" with both feet at the same time to expose seeds. When the female builds a new nest for a second brood, the male often takes over feeding the first brood. Unlike many other sparrow species, Song Sparrows rarely flock together. A common host of the Brown-headed Cowbird.

male

female

House Sparrow
Passer domesticus

YEAR-ROUND

Size:	6" (15 cm)
Male:	Brown back with a gray belly and cap. Large black patch extending from the throat to the chest (bib). 1 white wing bar.
Female:	slightly smaller than the male, light brown with light eyebrows; lacks a bib and white wing bar
Juvenile:	similar to female
Nest:	cavity; female and male build a domed cup nest within; 2–3 broods per year
Eggs:	4–6; white with brown markings
Incubation:	10–12 days; female incubates
Fledging:	14–17 days; female and male feed the young
Migration:	non-migrator; moves around to find food
Food:	seeds, insects, fruit; comes to seed feeders
Compare:	The Chipping Sparrow (p. 103) has a rusty crown. Look for the black bib to identify the male House Sparrow and the clear breast to help identify the female.

Stan's Notes: One of the first birdsongs heard in cities in spring. A familiar city bird, nearly always in small flocks. Also found on farms. Introduced in 1850 from Europe to Central Park in New York. Now seen throughout North America. Related to old-world sparrows; not a relative of any sparrows in the U.S. An aggressive bird that will kill young birds in order to take over the nest cavity. Uses dried grass and small scraps of plastic, paper, and other materials to build an oversize, domed nest in the cavity.

male
p. 281

female

Purple Finch
Haemorhous purpureus

YEAR-ROUND

Size: 6" (15 cm)

Female: Plain brown with heavy streaking on the chest. Bold white eyebrows and a large bill.

Male: raspberry-red head, cap, breast, back, and rump; brownish wings and tail

Juvenile: same as female

Nest: cup; female and male build; 1 brood per year

Eggs: 4–5; greenish blue with brown markings

Incubation: 12–13 days; female incubates

Fledging: 13–14 days; female and male feed the young

Migration: non-migrator to irruptive; moves around in winter to find food

Food: seeds, insects, fruit; comes to seed feeders

Compare: The female House Finch (p. 109) lacks eyebrows. The Pine Siskin (p. 107) has yellow wing bars. The female American Goldfinch (p. 305) has a clear chest. Look for the bold white eyebrows to identify the female Purple Finch.

Stan's Notes: A year-round resident throughout Maine. Has been replaced in cities by House Finches. Travels in flocks of up to 50 birds. Visits seed feeders along with House Finches, which makes it hard to tell them apart. Feeds mainly on seeds; ash tree seeds are an important source of food. Found in coniferous forests, mixed woods, woodland edges, and suburban backyards. Flies in the typical undulating, up-and-down pattern of finches. Sings a rich, loud song. Gives a distinctive "tic" note only in flight. The male is not purple. The Latin species name *purpureus* means "purple" (and other reddish colors).

white-striped

tan-striped

White-throated Sparrow
Zonotrichia albicollis

**YEAR-ROUND
SUMMER**

Size: 6–7" (15–18 cm)

Male: Brown with a gray or tan chest and belly and a white or tan throat patch and eyebrows. Bold striping on the head. Small yellow spot in the space between the eye and bill, called the lore.

Female: same as male

Juvenile: similar to adults, with a heavily streaked chest and a gray throat and eyebrows

Nest: cup; female builds; 1 brood per year

Eggs: 4–6; green to blue, or cream-white with red-brown markings

Incubation: 11–14 days; female incubates

Fledging: 10–12 days; female and male feed the young

Migration: non-migrator to complete, to southern states

Food: insects, seeds, fruit; visits ground feeders

Compare: The White-crowned Sparrow (p. 127) lacks the throat patch and yellow lores of the White-throated Sparrow. The Song Sparrow (p. 117) has a central spot on the chest and lacks the striped pattern on the head.

Stan's Notes: Two color variations (polymorphic): white striped and tan striped. Studies indicate that the white-striped adults tend to mate with the tan-striped birds; it's not clear why. Known for its wonderful song; it sings all year and can even be heard at night. White- and tan-striped males and white-striped females sing, but tan-striped females do not. Feeds on the ground under feeders. Often associated with other sparrows during winter. Nests are built on the ground underneath small trees in bogs and coniferous forests.

Fox Sparrow
Passerella iliaca

SUMMER
MIGRATION

Size: 7" (18 cm)

Male: Plump, rust-red sparrow. Heavily streaked rusty breast and solid-rust tail. Head and back are mottled with gray.

Female: same as male

Juvenile: same as adults

Nest: cup; female builds; 1 brood per year

Eggs: 2–4; pale green with reddish markings

Incubation: 12–14 days; female incubates

Fledging: 10–11 days; female and male feed the young

Migration: complete, to southern states

Food: seeds, insects; comes to ground feeders

Compare: The Brown Thrasher (p. 159) is much larger, is slimmer and has a long, curved bill. The rust-red plumage of the Fox Sparrow differentiates it from all other sparrows.

Stan's Notes: One of the largest sparrows. Often seen alone or in small groups. Found in shrubby areas, open fields, and backyards. Comes to ground feeders; searches for seeds and insects underneath seed feeders during migration. Like a chicken, it will "double-scratch" with both feet at the same time to look for food. Gives a series of rich notes lasting 2–3 seconds, usually singing from a perch hidden in a shrub. The common name "Sparrow" comes from the Anglo-Saxon word *spearwa*, meaning "flutterer," as applies to any small bird. "Fox" refers to its rusty color. Appears in several color variations, depending on location. Nests on the ground in brush and along forest edges.

juvenile

White-crowned Sparrow
Zonotrichia leucophrys

MIGRATION

Size: 6½–7½" (16.5–19 cm)

Male: Brown with a gray chest and black-and-white striped crown. Small, thin, yellow bill.

Female: same as male

Juvenile: similar to adults, with black and brown stripes on the head

Nest: cup; female builds; 2 broods per year

Eggs: 3–5; greenish to bluish to whitish with red-brown markings

Incubation: 11–14 days; female incubates

Fledging: 8–12 days; male and female feed the young

Migration: complete, to southern states and Mexico

Food: insects, seeds, berries; visits ground feeders

Compare: The White-throated Sparrow (p. 123) has a throat patch and a small yellow spot by each eye. The Song Sparrow (p. 117) has a streaked chest. Look for the striped crown to help identify the White-crowned Sparrow.

Stan's Notes: Often seen in groups of up to 20 birds during migration, when it can be seen visiting ground feeders and feeding beneath seed feeders. This ground feeder will "double-scratch" backward with both feet simultaneously to find seeds. Prefers scrubby areas, woodland edges, and open or grassy habitats. Males arrive at the breeding grounds before the females and sing from perches to establish territory. Males take most of the responsibility for raising the young while females start their second broods. Only 9–12 days separate the broods. Nests in Canada and Alaska.

Swainson's Thrush
Catharus ustulatus

SUMMER

Size: 7" (18 cm)

Male: Dusty-brown head, back, and wings. Brown smudges and spots, especially beneath chin, on the chest and on an off-white belly. Small, thin two-toned bill, yellow under and black above.

Female: same as male

Juvenile: similar to adult, less distinct spots on chest

Nest: cup; female builds; 1 brood per year

Eggs: 3–5; pale blue with brown markings

Incubation: 12–14 days; female incubates

Fledging: 10–14 days; female and male feed young

Migration: complete, to Mexico, Central America, and South America

Food: insects, fruit

Compare: American Robin (p. 239) is similar in shape, but it is larger and has a red breast and a gray head and back.

Stan's Notes: A summer resident that is more conspicuous during spring and fall migrations. The most common of the thrush species in the state. Often hard to see because most of the time it stays on the ground in thick vegetation. Song sounds like someone playing a flute. Feeds mostly on insects in spring and summer, adding fruit to its diet in late summer. Nests in shrubs or low in conifer trees, building a bulky cup nest consisting of grass, bark, and moss, all glued together with mud.

female

male
p. 25

Eastern Towhee
Pipilo erythrophthalmus

SUMMER

Size: 7–8" (18–20 cm)

Female: Mostly light-brown bird. Rusty red-brown sides and a white belly. Long brown tail with a white tip. Short, stout, pointed bill and rich-red eyes. White wing patches flash in flight.

Male: similar to female but black instead of brown

Juvenile: light brown with heavily streaked head, chest and belly, a long dark tail with a white tip

Nest: cup; female builds; 2 broods per year

Eggs: 3–4; cream-white with brown markings

Incubation: 12–13 days; female incubates

Fledging: 10–12 days; male and female feed young

Migration: complete, southern states, South America

Food: insects, seeds, fruit; visits ground feeders

Compare: Smaller than the American Robin (p. 239), which has a red breast and lacks the white belly. The female Rose-breasted Grosbeak (p. 135) has a heavily streaked breast and obvious white eyebrows.

Stan's Notes: Named for its distinctive "tow-hee" call, given by both sexes, but known mostly for its other characteristic call, which sounds like "drink-your-tea!" Will hop backward with both feet (double-scratching), raking up leaf litter to locate insects and seeds. The female does the brooding. The male feeds the young most of the time. In southern coastal states, some have red eyes; others have white eyes.

female

male

Horned Lark
Eremophila alpestris

YEAR-ROUND SUMMER

Size: 7–8" (18–20 cm)

Male: Tan to brown with black markings on the face. Black necklace and bill. Pale-yellow chin. Two tiny feather "horns" on the top of the head, sometimes hard to see. Dark tail with white outer tail feathers, seen in flight.

Female: duller than male; less noticeable "horns"

Juvenile: lacks a yellow chin and black markings; does not develop "horns" until the second year

Nest: ground; female builds; 2–3 broods per year

Eggs: 3–4; gray with brown markings

Incubation: 11–12 days; female incubates

Fledging: 9–12 days; female and male feed the young

Migration: non-migrator to partial in Maine; moves around to find food

Food: seeds, insects

Compare: The Eastern Meadowlark (p. 325) has a yellow breast and belly. Look for the black markings by the eyes and the black necklace to identify the Horned Lark.

Stan's Notes: The only true lark native to North America. A bird of open ground. Common in rural areas; often seen in large flocks. The population increased in North America over the past century as more land was cleared for farming. Male performs a fluttering courtship flight high in the air while singing a high-pitched song. Female performs a fluttering distraction display when the nest is disturbed. Starts breeding early in the year. Able to renest about a week after the brood fledges. Moves around in winter to find food. "Lark" comes from the Middle English *laverock*, or "a lark."

male
p. 49

female

Rose-breasted Grosbeak

Pheucticus ludovicianus

Size: 7–8" (18–20 cm)

Female: Plump and heavily streaked. Large, obvious white eyebrows. Large ivory bill. Orange-to-yellow wing linings.

Male: black and white with a triangular rose patch in the center of the chest, rose wing linings

Juvenile: similar to female

Nest: cup; female and male construct; 1–2 broods per year

Eggs: 3–5; blue-green with brown markings

Incubation: 13–14 days; female and male incubate

Fledging: 9–12 days; female and male feed the young

Migration: complete, to Mexico, Central America, and South America

Food: insects, seeds, fruit; comes to seed feeders

Compare: Looks like a large finch with bold white eyebrows and heavy streaking. The female Purple Finch (p. 121) has smaller eyebrows. The female House Finch (p. 109) lacks eyebrows.

Stan's Notes: Seen in small groups during spring migration. Prefers a mature deciduous forest for nesting. Both sexes sing, but the male sings much louder and clearer. Sings a rich, robin-like song with a chip note in the tune. "Grosbeak" refers to the thick, strong bill, which is used to crush seeds. Males arrive at the breeding grounds a few days before females. Several males will visit seed feeders together in spring. When females arrive, males become territorial and reduce their feeder visits. After fledging, the young visit feeders with the adults. Makes short flights from tree to tree with rapid wingbeats.

male
p. 27

female

Brown-headed Cowbird

Molothrus ater

SUMMER

Size: 7½" (19 cm)

Female: Dull brown with no obvious markings. Pointed, sharp, gray bill. Dark eyes.

Male: glossy black with a chocolate-brown head

Juvenile: similar to female but with dull-gray plumage and a streaked chest

Nest: no nest; lays eggs in the nests of other birds

Eggs: 5–7; white with brown markings

Incubation: 10–13 days; host birds incubate the eggs

Fledging: 10–11 days; host birds feed the young

Migration: complete, to southern states

Food: insects, seeds; will come to seed feeders

Compare: The female Red-winged Blackbird (p. 149) has white eyebrows and heavy streaking. The female Indigo Bunting (p. 113) has faint blue on its wings. The European Starling (p. 29) has speckles and a shorter tail. The pointed gray bill helps to identify the female Brown-headed Cowbird.

Stan's Notes: Cowbirds are members of the blackbird family. Known as brood parasites, Brown-headed Cowbirds are the only parasitic birds in the state. Brood parasites lay their eggs in the nests of other birds, leaving the host birds to raise their young. Cowbirds are known to have laid their eggs in the nests of over 200 species of birds. While some birds reject cowbird eggs, most incubate them and raise the young, even to the exclusion of their own. Look for warblers and other birds feeding young birds twice their own size. Named "Cowbird" for its habit of following bison and cattle herds to feed on insects flushed up by the animals.

1 year
old

Bohemian
Waxwing

Cedar Waxwing
Bombycilla cedrorum

YEAR-ROUND
SUMMER

Size: 7½" (19 cm)

Male: Sleek-looking, gray-to-brown bird. Pointed crest, bandit-like mask, and light-yellow belly. Bold-yellow tip of tail. Red wing tips look like they were dipped in red wax.

Female: same as male

Juvenile: grayish with a heavily streaked breast; lacks the sleek look, black mask, and red wing tips

Nest: cup; female and male construct; 1 brood per year, occasionally 2

Eggs: 4–6; pale blue with brown markings

Incubation: 10–12 days; female incubates

Fledging: 14–18 days; female and male feed the young

Migration: non-migrator to partial migrator; moves around to find food

Food: cedar cones, fruit, seeds, insects

Compare: The female Northern Cardinal (p. 147) has a large red bill. The Bohemian Waxwing (inset), is larger and less common and has white on its wings and rust under its tail. Look for the red wing tips to identify the Cedar Waxwing.

Stan's Notes: The name is derived from its red, wax-like wing tips and preference for the small, berry-like cones of the cedar. Seen in flocks, moving around from area to area looking for berries. Feeds on insects during summer, before berries are abundant. Wanders during winter, searching for food supplies. Spends most of its time at the top of tall trees. Listen for the high-pitched "sreee" whistling sound it constantly makes while perched or in flight. Obtains the mask after the first year and red wing tips after the second year.

Wood Thrush
Hylocichla mustelina

SUMMER

Size: 8" (20 cm)

Male: Reddish-brown head, back, and wings with color fading into a brown tail. A distinctive white breast, belly, and sides, covered with black spots. White ring around black eyes, obvious on a black-streaked white face.

Female: same as male

Juvenile: similar to adult

Nest: cup; female builds; 1–2 broods per year

Eggs: 2–4; greenish blue without markings

Incubation: 13–14 days; female incubates

Fledging: 11–12 days; female and male feed the young

Migration: complete, to Central and South America

Food: insects, fruit

Compare: American Robin (p. 239) is a similar body shape, but it has a red breast. Brown Thrasher (p. 159) is a similar rusty color, but it has a much longer rusty-red tail and bright-yellow eyes in comparison to the shorter brown tail and black eyes of Wood Thrush.

Stan's Notes: An easy thrush to identify due to the large dark spots on breast and belly. Well known for its liquid flute-like calls, heard deep within woodlots throughout Maine. Returns to the same woodlands during the last half of March. Often seen on the ground, hopping around like a robin in search of insects.

winter

breeding

Spotted Sandpiper
Actitis macularius

SUMMER

Size:	8" (20 cm)
Male:	Olive-brown back with black spots on a white chest and belly. White line over eyes. Long, dull-yellow legs. Long bill. Winter plumage lacks spots on the chest and belly.
Female:	female slightly larger
Juvenile:	similar to winter plumage, with a darker bill
Nest:	ground; male builds; 2 broods per year
Eggs:	3–4; brownish with brown markings
Incubation:	20–24 days; male incubates
Fledging:	17–21 days; male feeds the young
Migration:	complete, to southern coastal states, Mexico, and Central and South America
Food:	aquatic insects
Compare:	The Greater Yellowlegs (p. 169) is much larger. The Killdeer (p. 157) has 2 black neck bands. Look for the black spots on the chest and belly and the bobbing tail to help identify the breeding Spotted Sandpiper.

Stan's Notes: Seen along the shorelines of large ponds, lakes, and rivers. One of the few shorebirds that will dive underwater when pursued. Able to fly straight up out of the water. Holds wings in a cup-like arc in flight, rarely lifting them above a horizontal plane. Walks as if delicately balanced. When standing, constantly bobs its tail. Gives a rapid series of "weet-weet-weet" calls when frightened and flying away. Female mates with multiple males and lays eggs in up to five nests. Male does all of the nest building, incubating and childcare without any help from the female.

Northern Saw-whet Owl
Aegolius acadicus

YEAR-ROUND

Size: 8" (20 cm); up to 17" wingspan

Male: Small tawny brown with wide vertical rusty brown streaks on a white breast and belly. Distinctive light marks on back and wings. Short tail. A white face, yellow eyes, and small dark bill.

Female: same as male

Juvenile: dark brown; light brown belly

Nest: cavity; former woodpecker cavity; does not add any nesting material; 1 brood per year

Eggs: 5–6; white without markings

Incubation: 26–28 days; female and male incubate

Fledging: 27–34 days; male and female feed the young

Migration: partial to non-migrator

Food: mice, small birds, insects

Compare: The Barred Owl (p. 201) is larger and has dark eyes. The Great Horned Owl (p. 203) is much larger, with large and obvious ear tufts, which the Saw-whet lacks.

Stan's Notes: A resident throughout Maine, moving about in fall to the southern portion of the state. Our smallest owl, it is not often recognized as an owl because of its diminutive size. Usually found in mixed coniferous-deciduous forest. Strictly a nighttime hunter. Often roosts in cavities in conifers, thick vegetation, or Wood Duck nesting boxes. Has relatively long wings for such a small raptor. The common name comes from its rarely heard call, a repeated low raspy whistle that is reminiscent of a saw blade being sharpened. Can be very tame and approachable.

male
p. 285

female

juvenile

Northern Cardinal
Cardinalis cardinalis

YEAR-ROUND

Size: 8–9" (20–23 cm)

Female: Buff-brown with red tinges on the crest and wings. Black mask and a large reddish bill.

Male: red with a large crest and bill and a black mask extending from the face to the throat

Juvenile: same as female but with a blackish-gray bill

Nest: cup; female builds; 2–3 broods per year

Eggs: 3–4; bluish white with brown markings

Incubation: 12–13 days; female and male incubate

Fledging: 9–10 days; female and male feed the young

Migration: non-migrator

Food: seeds, insects, fruit; comes to seed feeders

Compare: The Cedar Waxwing (p. 139) has a small dark bill. The juvenile Northern Cardinal (bottom inset) looks like the adult female but with a dark bill. Look for the reddish bill to identify the female Northern Cardinal.

Stan's Notes: A familiar backyard bird. Seen in a variety of habitats, including parks. Usually likes thick vegetation. One of the few species in which both females and males sing. Can be heard all year. Listen for its "whata-cheer-cheer-cheer" territorial call in spring. Watch for a male feeding a female during courtship. The male also feeds the young of the first brood while the female builds a second nest. Territorial in spring, fighting its own reflection in a window or other reflective surface. Non-territorial in winter, gathering in small flocks of up to 20 birds. *Cardinalis* denotes importance, as represented by the red priestly garments of Catholic cardinals.

male
p. 31

female

Red-winged Blackbird
Agelaius phoeniceus

SUMMER

Size:	8½" (21.5 cm)
Female:	Heavily streaked brown body. Pointed brown bill and white eyebrows.
Male:	jet black with red-and-yellow shoulder patches (epaulets) and a pointed black bill
Juvenile:	same as female
Nest:	cup; female builds; 1–2 broods per year
Eggs:	3–4; bluish green with brown markings
Incubation:	10–12 days; female incubates
Fledging:	11–14 days; female and male feed the young
Migration:	complete, to southern states
Food:	seeds, insects; visits seed and suet feeders
Compare:	The female Rusty Blackbird (p. 237) is larger. The female Rose-breasted Grosbeak (p. 135) is plumper and has a thicker bill. The female Brown-headed Cowbird (p. 137) lacks streaks. Look for white eyebrows and heavy streaking to identify the female Red-winged.

Stan's Notes: One of the most widespread and numerous birds in Maine. Found around marshes, wetlands, lakes, and rivers. It is a sure sign of spring when these birds return to the marshes. Flocks with as many as 10,000 birds have been reported. Males arrive before females and sing to defend their territory. The male repeats his call from the top of a cattail while showing off his red-and-yellow shoulder patches. The female chooses a mate and often builds her nest over shallow water in a thick stand of cattails. The male can be aggressive when defending the nest. Feeds mostly on seeds in spring and fall, and insects throughout the summer.

female

male

Common Nighthawk

Chordeiles minor

SUMMER

Size: 9" (23 cm)

Male: Camouflaged brown and white with a white chin. Distinctive white band across the wings and tail, seen only in flight.

Female: similar to male, with a tan chin; lacks a white tail band

Juvenile: similar to female

Nest: no nest; lays eggs on the ground, usually on rocks or a rooftop; 1 brood per year

Eggs: 2; cream with brown and lavender markings

Incubation: 19–20 days; female incubates

Fledging: 20–21 days; female and male feed the young

Migration: complete, to South America

Food: insects caught in the air

Compare: The Chimney Swift (p. 101) is much smaller. The male Whip-poor-will (p. 153) is similar in size, but browner. Look for the obvious white band on the wings and characteristic flap-flap-flap-glide pattern to help identify the Common Nighthawk.

Stan's Notes: Usually only seen in flight at dusk or after sunset but not uncommon to see it sleeping on a branch during the day. A prolific insect eater and very noisy in flight, repeating a "peenting" call. Alternates slow wingbeats with bursts of quick wingbeats. In cities, prefers to nest on flat rooftops with gravel. City populations are on the decline as gravel rooftops are converted to other styles. In spring, the male performs a showy mating ritual consisting of a steep diving flight ending with a loud popping noise. One of the first birds to migrate in fall. Seen in large flocks, all heading south.

Whip-poor-will
Antrostomus vociferus

Size: 10" (25 cm)

Male: Mottled brown and black. Distinctive black chin and a white U-shaped throat marking.

Female: same as male, but has a brown chin and tan throat marking

Juvenile: similar to adult of the same sex

Nest: no nest; lays eggs on the ground; 1–2 broods per year

Eggs: 2; white with brown markings

Incubation: 19–20 days; female and male incubate

Fledging: 18–20 days; female and male feed the young

Migration: complete, to Mexico, Central America, and South America

Food: insects

Compare: Male Common Nighthawk (p. 151) has a distinctive white band across wings (seen in flight), which the Whip-poor-will lacks. Nighthawk is commonly seen flying, while Whip-poor-will is rarely seen flying.

Stan's Notes: A very well-known bird in Maine, although rarely seen. Its repetitive nocturnal "whip-poor-will" call, usually heard only in the spring, is loved by many and hated by others. Nothing can be done to stop the nocturnal calling despite how much sleep you are losing. Generally found in woodlands, Whip-poor-wills sit parallel on a branch during the day. They don't build nests but lay eggs on the ground, selecting sites along forest edges. The male will care for its young if the female starts a second brood.

in flight

juvenile

male

female

in-flight
juvenile

American Kestrel
Falco sparverius

SUMMER

Size: 9–11" (23–28 cm); up to 2' wingspan

Male: Rust-brown back and tail. White breast with dark spots. 2 vertical black lines on a white face. Blue-gray wings. Wide black band with a white edge on the tip of a rusty tail.

Female: similar to male but slightly larger, with rust-brown wings and dark bands on the tail

Juvenile: same as adult of the same sex

Nest: cavity; does not build a nest; 1 brood per year

Eggs: 4–5; white with brown markings

Incubation: 29–31 days; male and female incubate

Fledging: 30–31 days; female and male feed the young

Migration: partial to complete migrator

Food: insects, small mammals and birds, reptiles

Compare: The Peregrine Falcon (p. 257) is much larger and has a dark "hood" marking. No other small bird of prey has a rusty back and tail.

Stan's Notes: Most migrate, but some remain in urban settings in Maine, feeding on mice along roads. An unusual raptor because the sexes look different (dimorphic). Due to its small size, this falcon was once called a Sparrow Hawk. Hovers near roads, then dives for prey. Watch for it to pump its tail after landing on a perch. Perches nearly upright. Eats many grasshoppers. Hovers near roads before diving for prey. Adapts quickly to a wooden nest box. Has pointed swept-back wings, seen in flight. Can be extremely vocal, giving a loud series of high-pitched calls. Ability to see ultraviolet (UV) light helps it locate mice and other prey by their urine, which glows bright yellow in UV light.

SUMMER

Killdeer
Charadrius vociferus

Size: 11" (28 cm)

Male: Upland shorebird with 2 black bands around the neck, like a necklace. Brown back and white belly. Bright reddish-orange rump, visible in flight.

Female: same as male

Juvenile: similar to adults, with a single neck band

Nest: ground; male scrapes; 2 broods per year

Eggs: 3–5; tan with brown markings

Incubation: 24–28 days; male and female incubate

Fledging: 25 days; male and female lead their young to food

Migration: complete, to southern states, Mexico, and Central America

Food: insects, worms, snails

Compare: The Spotted Sandpiper (p. 143) is found around water and lacks the 2 neck bands of the Killdeer.

Stan's Notes: Technically classified as a shorebird but lives in dry habitats instead of the shore. Often found in vacant fields, gravel pits, driveways, wetland edges, or along railroad tracks. The only shorebird that has two black neck bands. Known to fake a broken wing to draw intruders away from the nest; once the nest is safe, the parent will take flight. Nests are just a slight depression in a dry area and are often hard to see. Hatchlings look like miniature adults walking on stilts. Soon after hatching, the young follow their parents around and peck for insects. Gives a loud and distinctive "kill-deer" call. Migrates in small flocks.

Brown Thrasher
Toxostoma rufum

SUMMER

Size: 11" (28 cm)

Male: Rust-red with a long tail. Heavy streaking on the breast and belly. 2 white wing bars. Long, curved bill and bright-yellow eyes.

Female: same as male

Juvenile: same as adults but with grayish eyes

Nest: cup; female and male build; 2 broods per year

Eggs: 4–5; pale blue with brown markings

Incubation: 11–14 days; female and male incubate

Fledging: 10–13 days; female and male feed the young

Migration: complete, to southern states

Food: insects, fruit

Compare: American Robin (p. 239) and Gray Catbird (p. 235) are similar but smaller and lack a streaked chest, rusty color, and yellow eyes. The Fox Sparrow (p. 125) has a similar rust-red coloration, but the Thrasher is much larger, is thinner, and has a longer bill and tail.

Stan's Notes: A prodigious songster. Often found in thick shrubs, where it will sing deliberate musical phrases, repeating each twice. The male Brown Thrasher has the largest documented repertoire of all North American songbirds, with more than 1,100 types of songs. Builds nest low in dense shrubs, often in fencerows. Quickly flies or runs on the ground in and out of thick shrubs. A noisy feeder due to its habit of turning over leaves, small rocks, and branches to find food. More abundant in the central Great Plains than anywhere else in North America.

male

female

Northern Flicker
Colaptes auratus

YEAR-ROUND
SUMMER

Size: 12" (30 cm)

Male: Brown and black with a black mustache and black necklace. Red spot on the nape of the neck. Speckled chest. Large white rump patch, seen only when flying.

Female: same as male but without a black mustache

Juvenile: same as adult of the same sex

Nest: cavity; female and male excavate; 1 brood per year

Eggs: 5–8; white without markings

Incubation: 11–14 days; female and male incubate

Fledging: 25–28 days; female and male feed the young

Migration: complete, to southern states; non-migrator in parts of Maine

Food: insects (especially ants and beetles); comes to suet feeders

Compare: The male Yellow-bellied Sapsucker (p. 51) has a red chin. The male Red-bellied Woodpecker (p. 57) has a red crown. Flickers are the only brown-backed woodpeckers in the state.

Stan's Notes: This is the only woodpecker to regularly feed on the ground. Prefers ants and beetles and produces an antacid saliva that neutralizes the acidic defense of ants. The male often picks the nest site. Parents take up to 12 days to excavate the cavity. Can be attracted to your yard with a nest box stuffed with sawdust. Often reuses an old nest. Undulates deeply during flight, flashing yellow under its wings and tail and calling "wacka-wacka" loudly.

Mourning Dove
Zenaida macroura

**YEAR-ROUND
SUMMER**

Size: 12" (30 cm)

Male: Smooth and fawn-colored. Gray patch on the head. Iridescent pink and greenish blue on the neck. Black spot behind and below the eyes. Black spots on the wings and tail. Pointed, wedged tail; white edges seen in flight.

Female: similar to male, but lacks the pink-and-green iridescent neck feathers

Juvenile: spotted and streaked plumage

Nest: platform; female and male build; 2 broods per year

Eggs: 2; white without markings

Incubation: 13–14 days; male incubates during the day, female incubates at night

Fledging: 12–14 days; female and male feed the young

Migration: non-migrator to partial migrator, to southern states; moves around the state to find food

Food: seeds; will visit ground and seed feeders

Compare: Eurasian Collared-Dove (p. 247) has a black collar on the nape of its neck. Rock Pigeon (p. 249) is larger and has a wide range of color combinations.

Stan's Notes: Name comes from its mournful cooing. A ground feeder, bobbing its head as it walks. One of the few birds to drink without lifting its head, like the Rock Pigeon. The parents feed the young (squab) a regurgitated liquid called crop-milk during their first few days of life. Platform nest is so flimsy it often falls apart in a storm. During takeoff and in flight, wind rushes through the bird's wing feathers, creating a characteristic whistling sound.

winter

breeding

Pied-billed Grebe
Podilymbus podiceps

SUMMER

Size: 12–14" (30–36 cm)

Male: Small and brown with a black chin and fluffy white patch beneath the tail. Black ring around a thick, chicken-like, ivory bill. Winter bill is brown and unmarked.

Female: same as male

Juvenile: paler than adults, with white spots and a gray chest, belly and bill

Nest: floating platform; female and male construct; 1 brood per year

Eggs: 5–7; bluish white without markings

Incubation: 22–24 days; female and male incubate

Fledging: 45–60 days; female and male feed the young

Migration: complete, to southern states, Mexico, and Central America

Food: crayfish, aquatic insects, fish

Compare: Look for the white patch under the tail and the thick bill to help identify the Pied-billed.

Stan's Notes: Very common waterbird, often seen diving for food. When disturbed, it slowly sinks like a submarine, quickly compressing its feathers, forcing the air out. Was called Hell-diver due to the length of time it can stay submerged. Able to surface far from where it went under. Well suited to life on water, with short wings, lobed toes, and legs set close to the rear of its body. Swims easily but moves awkwardly on land. Very sensitive to pollution. Builds nest on a floating mat in water. "Grebe" may originate from the Breton word *krib*, meaning "crest," referring to the crested head plumes of many grebes, especially during breeding season.

male
p. 63

female

Bufflehead
Bucephala albeola

MIGRATION
WINTER

Size: 13–15" (33–38 cm)

Female: Brownish-gray duck with a dark-brown head. White patch on cheek, just behind the eyes.

Male: striking black-and-white duck with a large bonnet-like white patch on the back of head; head shines greenish purple in sunlight

Juvenile: similar to female

Nest: cavity; female lines an old woodpecker cavity; 1 brood per year

Eggs: 8–10; ivory-to-olive without markings

Incubation: 29–31 days; female incubates

Fledging: 50–55 days; female leads the young to food

Migration: complete, along the East coast from Maine to Florida, Mexico, and Central America

Food: aquatic insects

Compare: Confused with the female Common Goldeneye (p. 193), which lacks the white cheek patch. Look for the white cheek patch to help identify the female Bufflehead.

Stan's Notes: A small, common diving duck. Usually seen during migration and winter, arriving late in August. Wintering in the southern half of Maine, in small groups or with other duck species in sheltered bays and coastal harbors. It is also seen inland on rivers, ponds, and lakes. Nests in vacant woodpecker holes. When cavities in trees are scarce, known to use a burrow in an earthen bank or will use a nest box. Lines the cavity with fluffy down feathers. Unlike other ducks, the young stay in the nest for up to two days before they venture out with their mothers. The female is very territorial and remains with the same mate for many years.

Greater Yellowlegs
Tringa melanoleuca

MIGRATION

Size: 13–15" (33–38 cm)

Male: Tall with a bulbous head and a long, thin, slightly upturned bill. Gray streaking on the chest. White belly. Long yellow legs.

Female: same as male

Juvenile: same as adults

Nest: ground; female builds; 1 brood per year

Eggs: 3–4; off-white with brown markings

Incubation: 22–23 days; female and male incubate

Fledging: 18–20 days; male and female feed the young

Migration: complete, to southern coastal states, and Central and South America

Food: small fish, aquatic insects

Compare: The breeding Willet (p. 171) is similar in size, not as brown. The Killdeer (p. 157) has 2 black bands around its neck. The breeding Spotted Sandpiper (p. 143) has spots on its chest. Look for the long yellow legs and long bill to identify the Greater Yellowlegs.

Stan's Notes: A common shorebird, usually seen during migration. Can be identified by its long legs, which enable it to wade in deep water, and its slightly upturned bill. Often seen resting on one leg. Rushes forward through the water to feed, plowing its bill or swinging it from side to side, catching small fish and insects. A skittish bird, it is quick to give an alarm call, causing flocks to take flight. Typically moves into the water before taking flight. Gives a variety of "flight" notes at takeoff. Nests on the ground close to water on the northern tundra of Labrador and Newfoundland.

breeding

winter
p. 253

displaying

Willet
Tringa semipalmatus

SUMMER

Size: 14–16" (36–40 cm)

Male: Brown breeding plumage with a white belly. Brown bill and legs. Distinctive black-and-white wing lining pattern, seen in flight or during display.

Female: same as male

Juvenile: similar to breeding adult, more tan in color

Nest: ground; female builds; 1 brood per year

Eggs: 3–5; olive-green with dark markings

Incubation: 24–28 days; male and female incubate

Fledging: 1–2 days; female and male feed young

Migration: complete, to southern coastal states, coastal Central and South America

Food: insects, small fish, crabs, worms, clams

Compare: Greater Yellowlegs (p. 169) is slightly smaller and has a smaller head, longer neck and yellow legs. Killdeer (p. 157) has 2 black bands on the neck.

Stan's Notes: A common summer coastal resident. It appears a rich, warm brown during the breeding season and rather plain gray during the winter, but it always has a striking black-and-white wing pattern when seen in flight. One of the few shorebirds that is seen away from water, sometimes standing on fence posts. Uses its black-and-white wing patches to display to its mate. Named after the "pill-will-willet" call it gives during the breeding season. Gives a "kip-kip-kip" alarm call when it takes flight. Nests along the Gulf and East Coasts, in some western states and Canada.

male

female

Green-winged Teal
Anas crecca

YEAR-ROUND
SUMMER

Size: 14–15" (36–38 cm)

Male: Chestnut head with a dark-green patch out-lined with white from the eyes to the nape of the neck. Gray body. Butter-yellow tail. Green patch on the wings (speculum), seen in flight.

Female: light brown with black spots and a green speculum; small bill

Juvenile: same as female

Nest: ground; female builds; 1 brood per year

Eggs: 8–10; cream-white without markings

Incubation: 21–23 days; female incubates

Fledging: 32–34 days; female teaches the young to feed

Migration: complete, to eastern coastal U.S., southern states, and Mexico; non-migrator in coastal Maine

Food: aquatic plants and insects

Compare: The male Green-winged Teal is not as colorful as the male Wood Duck (p. 267). The female Blue-winged Teal (p. 175) is similar in size, but it has slight white at the base of its bill. Look for the chestnut head with a dark-green patch on each side to identify the male Green-winged Teal.

Stan's Notes: One of the smallest dabbling ducks. Tips forward in water to feed off the bottom of shallow ponds. This behavior makes it vulnerable to ingesting spent lead shot, which can cause death. It walks well on land and will also feed in flooded fields and woodlands. Known for its fast and agile flight. Groups wheel and spin through the air in tight formation. The green wing patches are most obvious during flight.

173

male

female

Blue-winged Teal
Spatula discors

SUMMER

Size: 15–16" (38–41 cm)

Male: Small, plain-looking brown duck with black speckles and a large, crescent-shaped white mark at the base of the bill. Gray head. Black tail with a small white patch. Blue wing patch (speculum), best seen in flight.

Female: duller than male, with only slight white at the base of the bill; lacks a crescent mark on the face and a white patch on the tail

Juvenile: same as female

Nest: ground; female builds; 1 brood per year

Eggs: 8–11; cream-white

Incubation: 23–27 days; female incubates

Fledging: 35–44 days; female feeds the young

Migration: complete, to southern states, Mexico, and Central America

Food: aquatic plants, seeds, aquatic insects

Compare: Female Green-winged Teal (p. 173) lacks white near its bill. The female Mallard (p. 197) has an orange-and-black bill. The female Wood Duck (p. 191) has a crest. Look for the white facial mark to identify the male Blue-winged.

Stan's Notes: This is one of the smallest ducks in North America. An early migrator in Maine, arriving shortly after lakes are free of ice. A widespread nester that breeds as far north as Alaska. Constructs nest some distance from the water. Female performs a distraction display to protect the nest and young. Male leaves the female near the end of incubation. One of the longest-distance migrating ducks. Planting crops and cultivating to pond edges have caused declining populations.

male

female

Spruce Grouse
Falcipennis canadensis

YEAR-ROUND

Size: 16" (40 cm)

Male: Plump grouse, brown to almost black, with white speckles on the chest and belly. Short neck, red eyebrows (combs), and short dark tail with chestnut tip. Displaying male fans tail, leans forward and droops wings while quickly flapping wings in a short flight.

Female: overall brown with small black and white barring on the chest, dark brown tail with chestnut tip

Juvenile: same as female

Nest: ground; female builds; 1 brood per year

Eggs: 4–7; tan with brown markings

Incubation: 17–24 days; female incubates

Fledging: 8–10 days; male and female feed the young

Migration: non-migrator

Food: insect, seeds, berries

Compare: The Ruffed Grouse (p. 187) is slightly larger, lighter brown and has a tuft of feathers on head and tail that is not as dark.

Stan's Notes: Well known for being semi-tame and approachable. In winter it is often seen in groups along roads, where snow isn't as deep and small rocks can be eaten to aid in digestion. Prefers open coniferous forest. Roosts in trees. The females are territorial against other females. Cryptic coloring of female allows her to blend in with surroundings. Often freezes when danger approaches, hence its other common name, Fool Hen.

male p. 65

female

Lesser Scaup
Aythya affinis

MIGRATION

Size: 16–17" (40–43 cm)

Female: Overall brown duck with a dull-white patch at the base of a light-gray bill. Yellow eyes.

Male: white and gray; the chest and head appear nearly black but the head looks purple with green highlights in direct sun; yellow eyes

Juvenile: same as female

Nest: ground; female builds; 1 brood per year

Eggs: 8–14; olive-buff without markings

Incubation: 22–28 days; female incubates

Fledging: 45–50 days; female teaches young to feed

Migration: complete, to southern states, Mexico, Central America, and northern South America

Food: aquatic plants and insects

Compare: The male Blue-winged Teal (p. 175) is slightly smaller and has a crescent-shaped white mark at the base of its bill. The female Ring-necked Duck is similar in size, but lacks the white ring around the bill. The female Wood Duck (p. 191) is larger with white around the eyes.

Stan's Notes: Common migrating diving duck in Maine. Often in large flocks on lakes, ponds, and sewage lagoons during migration. Submerges itself completely to feed on the bottom of lakes (unlike dabbling ducks, which only tip forward to reach the bottom). Note the bold white stripe under the wings when in flight. The male leaves the female when she starts incubating eggs. This species has an interesting babysitting arrangement in which groups of young (crèches) are tended by one to three adult females. Prefers fresh water, but can be seen along the coast. Doesn't breed in Maine.

soaring

Broad-winged Hawk
Buteo platypterus

Size: 14–19" (36–48 cm); up to 3' wingspan

Male: Brown back and rust-red bars on the breast. 2 or 3 wide black-and-white tail bands. Short, round wings. White under the wings and black "fingertips," seen in flight.

Female: same as male but slightly larger

Juvenile: tail bands narrower and more numerous; brown-streaked chest and belly

Nest: platform; female and male build, but female finishes; 1 brood per year

Eggs: 2–3; off-white with brown markings

Incubation: 28–32 days; female incubates; male feeds the female during incubation

Fledging: 34–40 days; female and male feed the young

Migration: complete, to Central and South America

Food: small birds, small mammals, snakes, frogs, toads, large insects

Compare: Cooper's Hawk (p. 255) has a longer, thinner tail. The Sharp-shinned Hawk (p. 251) is much smaller. Look for the black-and-white tail bands to identify the Broad-winged.

Stan's Notes: A common woodland hawk in Maine. Seen in large groups (kettles) migrating in early fall. Spends most of its time hunting small birds, snakes, and frogs in dense woods. Short wings help it navigate around trees. Often heard before it is seen. Screams a high-pitched whistle call repetitively when intruders are near the nest. Performs a sky-dance courtship with steep dives, sharp flights upward and rolling over.

soaring

Red-shouldered Hawk

Buteo lineatus

SUMMER

Size: 15–19" (38–48 cm); up to 3½' wingspan

Male: Reddish (cinnamon) head, shoulders, breast, and belly. Wings and back are dark brown with white spots. Long tail with thin white bands and wide black bands. Obvious red wing linings, seen in flight.

Female: same as male

Juvenile: similar to adults but lacks the cinnamon color; white chest with dark spots

Nest: platform; female and male construct; 1 brood per year

Eggs: 2–4; white with dark markings

Incubation: 27–29 days; female and male incubate

Fledging: 39–45 days; female feeds the young

Migration: complete, to southern states

Food: reptiles, amphibians, large insects, birds

Compare: The Red-tailed Hawk (p. 199) has a white chest. The Sharp-shinned Hawk (p. 251) is smaller and lacks the reddish head and belly of the Red-shouldered Hawk.

Stan's Notes: Common woodland hawk in Maine. Seen in backyards. Likes to hunt at forest edges, spotting snakes, frogs, insects, occasional small birds, and other prey as it perches. Often flaps with an alternating gliding pattern. Very vocal with a distinct scream. Breeds when it reaches 2–3 years. Remains in the same territory for many years. Starts constructing its nest in March or April. Young leave the nest in June or July.

male
p. 67

female

Ring-necked Duck
Aythya collaris

SUMMER

Size:	16–19" (41–48 cm)
Female:	Brown with a darker brown back and crown and lighter-brown sides. Gray face. White eye-ring with a white line behind the eye. White ring around the bill. Peaked head.
Male:	black head, chest, and back; gray-to-white sides; blue bill with a bold white ring and a thinner ring at the base; peaked head
Juvenile:	similar to female
Nest:	ground; female builds; 1 brood per year
Eggs:	8–10; olive to brown without markings
Incubation:	26–27 days; female incubates
Fledging:	49–56 days; female teaches the young to feed
Migration:	complete, to southern states, West Indies, Mexico, and Central America
Food:	aquatic plants and insects
Compare:	The female Lesser Scaup (p. 179) is similar in size. Look for the white ring around the bill to help identify the female Ring-necked Duck.

Stan's Notes: A common breeding duck in Maine. Often seen in larger freshwater lakes, usually in small flocks or just pairs. A diving duck, watch for it to dive underwater to forage for food. Springs up off the water to take flight. Has a distinctive tall, peaked head with a sloped forehead. Flattens its crown when diving. Male gives a quick series of grating barks and grunts. Female gives high-pitched peeps. Named "Ring-necked" for its cinnamon collar, which is nearly impossible to see in the field. Also called Ring-billed Duck due to the white ring on its bill.

drumming

Ruffed Grouse
Bonasa umbellus

YEAR-ROUND

Size:	16–19" (41–48 cm); up to 2' wingspan
Male:	Brown chicken-like bird with a long, squared tail. Wide black band near tip of tail. Tuft of feathers on head (crest) appears like a crown when raised. Black ruffs on the sides of neck.
Female:	same as male, but has less obvious neck ruffs
Juvenile:	same as female
Nest:	ground; female builds; 1 brood per year
Eggs:	9–12; tan with light-brown markings
Incubation:	23–24 days; female incubates
Fledging:	10–12 days; female leads the young to food
Migration:	non-migrator; moves around to find food
Food:	seeds, insects, fruit, leaf buds
Compare:	The Spruce Grouse (p. 177) is slightly smaller and has a darker tail. Look for the feather tuft on the head and black neck ruffs to help identify the Ruffed Grouse.

Stan's Notes: A common bird of deep woods. Often seen in aspen or other trees, feeding on leaf buds. In the colder northern climates, scaly bristles grow on its feet during winter and serve as snowshoes. When there is enough snow, it dives into a snowbank to roost at night. In spring, the male attracts females by raising its feather tuft, fanning its tail like a turkey, and standing on a log, drumming with its wings. The drumming sound is not made by its wings pounding against its chest or hitting the log, but by the air being moved by its cupped wings. Female performs a distraction display to protect her young. Two color morphs, red and gray, most apparent in the tail. Named for the black ruffs on its neck.

female

male
p. 69

Hooded Merganser
Lophodytes cucullatus

YEAR-ROUND
SUMMER

Size: 16–19" (41–48 cm)

Female: Sleek brown-and-rust bird with a red head. Ragged "hair" on the back of the head. Long, thin, brown bill.

Male: black back, rust-brown sides, long black bill; raises crest "hood" to display a white patch

Juvenile: similar to female

Nest: cavity; female lines an old woodpecker cavity or a nest box near water; 1 brood per year

Eggs: 10–12; white without markings

Incubation: 32–33 days; female incubates

Fledging: 71 days; female feeds the young

Migration: complete, to coastal states and Mexico

Food: small fish, aquatic insects, crustaceans

Compare: The female Red-breasted Merganser (p. 207) is similar, but smaller and has a larger, lighter-colored bill. The female Common Merganser (p. 289) is much larger and has a white chin and orange bill. Larger than female Lesser Scaup (p. 179), which has a dull-white patch at base of bill. Look for the ragged "hair" on the back of the head to help identify the female Hoodie.

Stan's Notes: A small diving duck, found in shallow ponds, sloughs, lakes, and rivers. Usually in small groups. Quick, low flight across the water, with fast wingbeats. Male has a deep, rolling call. Female gives a hoarse quack. Nests in wooded areas. Female will lay some eggs in the nests of other mergansers, goldeneyes, or Wood Ducks (egg dumping), resulting in 20–25 eggs in some nests. Rarely, she shares a nest, sitting with a Wood Duck.

male
p. 267

female

Wood Duck

Aix sponsa

SUMMER

Size: 17–20" (43–51 cm)

Female: Small brown dabbling duck. Bright-white eye-ring and a not-so-obvious crest. Blue patch on wings (speculum), often hidden.

Male: highly ornamented, with a mostly green head and crest patterned with black and white; rusty chest, white belly and red eyes

Juvenile: similar to female

Nest: cavity; female lines an old woodpecker cavity or a nest box in a tree; 1–2 brood per year

Eggs: 10–15; cream-white without markings

Incubation: 28–36 days; female incubates

Fledging: 56–68 days; female teaches the young to feed

Migration: complete, to southern states

Food: aquatic insects, plants, seeds

Compare: The female Mallard (p. 197) is larger and the female Blue-winged Teal (p. 175) is similar to the female Wood Duck. The Mallard and Teal lack the female Duck's bright white eye-ring and crest.

Stan's Notes: A common duck of quiet, shallow backwater ponds. Nearly went extinct around 1900 due to overhunting, but it's doing well now. Nests in a tree cavity or a nest box in a tree. Seen flying in forests or perching on high branches. Female takes off with a loud, squealing call and enters the nest cavity from full flight. Lays some eggs in a neighboring nest (egg dumping), resulting in more than 20 eggs in some clutches. Hatchlings stay in the nest for 24 hours, then jump from as high as 60 feet (18 m) to the ground or water to follow their mother. They never return to the nest.

female

male
p. 71

Common Goldeneye
Bucephala clangula

YEAR-ROUND
WINTER

Size: 18–20" (45–51 cm)

Female: Brown-and-gray duck with a large dark-brown head and gray body. White collar. Bright-golden eyes. Yellow-tipped dark bill.

Male: mostly white with a black back, a puffy green head, a large white spot on the face, bright-golden eyes and a dark bill

Juvenile: same as female but with a dark bill

Nest: cavity; female lines an old woodpecker cavity; 1 brood per year

Eggs: 8–10; light green without markings

Incubation: 28–32 days; female incubates

Fledging: 56–59 days; female leads the young to food

Migration: partial to non-migrator in Maine

Food: aquatic plants, insects, fish, mollusks

Compare: Similar to female Lesser Scaup (p. 179), which is smaller. Look for the dark-brown head, white collar and golden-yellow eye to help identify the female Common Goldeneye.

Stan's Notes: Known for the loud whistling sound produced by its wings during flight. During late winter and early spring, the male performs elaborate mating displays that include throwing his head back and calling a raspy note. Female will lay some of her eggs in other goldeneye nests or in the nests of other species (egg dumping), causing some mothers to incubate as many as 30 eggs in a brood. Named for its bright-golden eyes. Moves to southern and coastal Maine during winter.

male
p. 259

female

male
p. 259

soaring

SUMMER

Northern Harrier
Circus hudsonius

Size: 18–22" (45–56 cm); up to 4' wingspan

Female: Slender, low-flying hawk with a dark-brown back and brown streaking on the chest and belly. Large white rump patch. Thin black tail bands and black wing tips. Yellow eyes.

Male: silver-gray with a large white rump patch and white belly, black wing tips, yellow eyes, faint, thin bands across the tail

Juvenile: similar to female, with an orange chest

Nest: ground; female and male construct; 1 brood per year

Eggs: 4–8; bluish white without markings

Incubation: 31–32 days; female incubates

Fledging: 30–35 days; male and female feed the young

Migration: complete, to southern states, Mexico, and Central America; winters in coastal Maine

Food: mice, snakes, insects, small birds

Compare: Slimmer than the Red-tailed Hawk (p. 199). Look for the characteristic low gliding and the black tail bands to identify the female Harrier.

Stan's Notes: One of the easiest of hawks to identify. Glides just above the ground, following the contours of the land while searching for prey. Holds its wings just above horizontal, tilting back and forth in the wind, similar to the Turkey Vulture. Formerly called Marsh Hawk due to its habit of hunting over marshes. Feeds and nests on the ground. Will also preen and rest on the ground. Unlike other hawks, mainly uses its hearing to find prey, followed by its sight. At any age, it has a distinctive owl-like face disk.

male
p. 269

female

Mallard
Anas platyrhynchos

YEAR-ROUND
SUMMER

Size: 19–21" (48–53 cm)

Female: Brown duck with a blue-and-white wing mark (speculum). Orange-and-black bill.

Male: large green head, white necklace, rust-brown or chestnut chest, combination of gray-and-white sides, yellow bill, orange legs and feet

Juvenile: same as female but with a yellow bill

Nest: ground; female builds; 1 brood per year

Eggs: 7–10; greenish to whitish, unmarked

Incubation: 26–30 days; female incubates

Fledging: 42–52 days; female leads the young to food

Migration: complete, to southern states; non-migrator in parts of Maine

Food: seeds, plants, aquatic insects; will come to ground feeders offering corn

Compare: The female Wood Duck (p. 191) has a white eye-ring. The female Blue-winged Teal (p. 175) is smaller than the female Mallard.

Stan's Notes: A familiar dabbling duck of lakes and ponds. Also found in rivers, streams, and some backyards. Tips forward to feed on vegetation on the bottom of shallow water. The name "Mallard" comes from the Latin word *masculus*, meaning "male," referring to the male's habit of taking no part in raising the young. Female and male have white underwings and white tails, but only the male has black central tail feathers that curl upward. The female gives a classic quack. Returns to its birthplace each year.

soaring

juvenile
soaring

juvenile

Red-tailed Hawk
Buteo jamaicensis

YEAR-ROUND
SUMMER

Size: 19–23" (48–58 cm); up to 4½' wingspan

Male: Variety of colorations, from chocolate brown to nearly all white. Often brown with a white breast and brown belly band. Rust-red tail. Underside of wing is white with a small dark patch on the leading edge near the shoulder.

Female: same as male but slightly larger

Juvenile: similar to adults, with a speckled breast and light eyes; lacks a red tail

Nest: platform; male and female construct; 1 brood per year

Eggs: 2–3; white without markings, sometimes marked with brown

Incubation: 30–35 days; female and male incubate

Fledging: 45–46 days; male and female feed the young

Migration: partial migrator to non-migrator; moves around to find food

Food: small and medium-size animals, large birds, snakes, fish, insects, bats, carrion

Compare: Broad-winged Hawk (p. 181), Cooper's Hawk (p. 255), Red-shouldered Hawk (p. 183), and Sharp-shinned Hawk (p. 251) are smaller and lack the red tail.

Stan's Notes: Common in open country and cities. Seen perching on fences, freeway lampposts, and trees. Look for it circling above open fields and roadsides, searching for prey. Gives a high-pitched scream that trails off. Often builds a large stick nest in large trees along roads. Lines nest with finer material, like evergreen needles. Returns to the same nest site each year. The red tail develops in the second year and is best seen from above.

Barred Owl
Strix varia

YEAR-ROUND

Size: 20–24" (51–61 cm); up to 3½' wingspan

Male: Chunky brown-and-gray owl with a large head and dark-brown eyes. Dark horizontal barring on upper chest. Vertical streaks on lower chest and belly. Yellow bill and feet.

Female: same as male but slightly larger

Juvenile: light gray with a black face

Nest: cavity; does not add nesting material; 1 brood per year

Eggs: 2–3; white without markings

Incubation: 28–33 days; female incubates

Fledging: 42–44 days; female and male feed the young

Migration: non-migrator

Food: mice, rabbits, and other animals; small birds; fish; reptiles; amphibians

Compare: Great Horned Owl (p. 203) has "horns." The Northern Saw-whet (p. 145) is less than half the size and has yellow eyes. Look for a stocky owl with a large head and dark-brown eyes to identify the Barred Owl.

Stan's Notes: A very common owl in the state. Prefers deciduous, dense woodlands with sparse undergrowth, but it can be attracted to your yard with a simple nest box that has a large entrance hole. Often seen hunting during the day. Perches and watches for mice, birds, and other prey. Hovers over water and reaches down to grab fish. After fledging, the young stay with their parents for up to four months. Often sounds like a dog barking just before calling 6—8 hoots, sounding like "who-who-who-cooks-for-you." The Great Horned Owl sounds like, "Hoo-hoo-hoo-hoooo!"

Great Horned Owl
Bubo virginianus

YEAR-ROUND

Size: 21–25" (53–64 cm); up to 4' wingspan

Male: Robust brown "horned" owl. Bright-yellow eyes and a V-shaped white throat resembling a necklace. Horizontal barring on the chest.

Female: same as male but slightly larger

Juvenile: similar to adults but lacks ear tufts

Nest: no nest; takes over the nest of a crow, hawk or Great Blue Heron or uses a partial cavity, stump or broken tree; 1 brood per year

Eggs: 2–3; white without markings

Incubation: 30–35 days; female incubates

Fledging: 30–35 days; male and female feed the young

Migration: non-migrator

Food: mammals, birds (ducks), snakes, insects

Compare: The Barred Owl (p. 201) has dark eyes and no "horns." The Northern Saw-whet Owl (p. 145) is a quarter the size. Look for bright-yellow eyes and feather "horns" on the head to help identify the Great Horned Owl.

Stan's Notes: The largest owl and one of the earliest-nesting birds in Maine, laying eggs in January and February. Can hear a mouse move beneath a foot of snow. The "horns," or "ears," are tufts of feathers and have nothing to do with hearing. Cannot turn its head all the way around. Wing feathers are ragged on the ends, resulting in silent flight. Eyelids close from the top down, like ours. Fearless, it is one of the few animals that will kill skunks and porcupines. Given that, it is also called the Flying Tiger. Call sounds like "hoo-hoo-hoo-hoooo."

male

female

American Black Duck

Anas rubripes

YEAR-ROUND
SUMMER

Size: 23" (58 cm)

Male: Overall dark brown, sometimes appearing nearly black, with a lighter head and neck. Violet patch on the wings (speculum), bordered with black. Dark wings contrast sharply with white wing linings, seen in flight. Yellow bill and orange legs.

Female: same as male, except bill is dull green with black flecks

Juvenile: same as female

Nest: ground; female builds; 1 brood per year

Eggs: 8–10; creamy white to greenish buff

Incubation: 26–29 days; female incubates

Fledging: 16–17 days; female teaches young to feed

Migration: complete, to southern states, non-migrator in parts of Maine

Food: aquatic plants and insects, seeds

Compare: Male and female American Black Ducks are very similar to the female Mallard (p. 197), but the female Mallard has an orange bill and a blue wing patch (speculum) bordered with white.

Stan's Notes: Was once one of the most abundant ducks breeding in the U.S. Mallards are more common now. Sometimes hybridizes (mates) with Mallards, producing a bird lacking the brilliant colors of the male Mallard. Female constructs a nest in grass that is high enough to conceal. Male leaves female while she is still incubating eggs. Young leave the nest 1–3 hours after hatching.

male
p. 271

female

Red-breasted Merganser
Mergus serrator

Size: 23" (58 cm)

Female: Overall brown-to-gray duck with a shaggy reddish head and crest. Long orange bill.

Male: shaggy green head and crest, a prominent white collar, rusty breast, black-and-white body, long orange bill

Juvenile: similar to female

Nest: ground; female builds; 1 brood per year

Eggs: 5–10; olive green without markings

Incubation: 29–30 days; female incubates

Fledging: 55–65 days; female feeds young

Migration: complete, to coastal Maine, southern coastal states, Central America, and Mexico

Food: fish, aquatic insects

Compare: The female Hooded Merganser (p. 189) is very similar, but it is smaller and has a smaller, darker bill.

Stan's Notes: A winter resident of far southwestern Maine, commonly seen on the coast. This duck is a very fast flier, clocked at up to 100 miles (161 km) per hour. Frequently seen flying low across the water. Needs a long run for takeoff with wings flapping to get airborne. Serrated bill helps it catch slippery fish. Usually is a silent duck. Male sometimes gives a soft, catlike meow. Female gives a harsh "krrr-croak." Doesn't breed before 2 years of age. The male abandons the female just after eggs are laid. Females often share nests. Breeds across Alaska, northern Canada, and inland Maine, wintering on the coast. The young leave the nest within 24 hours of hatching, never to return.

displaying male

non-displaying

female

Wild Turkey

Meleagris gallopavo

YEAR-ROUND

Size: 36–48" (91–122 cm)

Male: Large brown-and-bronze bird with a naked blue-and-red head. Long, straight, black beard in the center of the chest. Tail spreads open like a fan. Spurs on legs.

Female: thinner and less striking than the male; often lacks a breast beard

Juvenile: same as adult of the same sex

Nest: ground; female builds; 1 brood per year

Eggs: 10–12; buff-white with dull-brown markings

Incubation: 27–28 days; female incubates

Fledging: 6–10 days; female leads the young to food

Migration: non-migrator; moves around to find food

Food: insects, seeds, fruit

Compare: This bird is quite distinctive and unlikely to be confused with any other.

Stan's Notes: The largest native game bird in Maine, and the species from which the domestic turkey was bred. A strong flier that can approach 60 mph (97 kph). Can fly straight up, then away. Eyesight is three times better than ours. Hearing is also excellent; can hear competing males up to a mile away. Male has a "harem" of up to 20 females. Female scrapes out a shallow depression for nesting and pads it with soft leaves. Males are known as toms, females are hens, and young are poults. Roosts in trees at night. Eliminated in many areas due to market hunting and loss of habitat. Was reintroduced during the 1960s–1980s. Populations are now stable.

Ruby-crowned Kinglet
Regulus calendula

SUMMER

Size: 4" (10 cm)

Male: Small, teardrop-shaped green-to-gray bird. 2 white wing bars and a white eye-ring. Hidden ruby crown.

Female: same as male, but lacks a ruby crown

Juvenile: same as female

Nest: pendulous; female builds; 1 brood per year

Eggs: 4–5; white with brown markings

Incubation: 11–12 days; female incubates

Fledging: 11–12 days; female and male feed the young

Migration: complete, to southern states, Mexico, and Central America

Food: insects, seeds, berries

Compare: The Golden-crowned Kinglet (p. 213) is similar but lacks a ruby crown. The female American Goldfinch (p. 305) shares the drab olive plumage and unmarked chest, but it is larger. Look for the white eye-ring to identify the Ruby-crowned Kinglet.

Stan's Notes: One of the smaller birds in Maine. A summer resident, but is most commonly seen during spring and summer migrations, when groups travel together. Watch for it flitting in thick shrubs low to the ground. It takes a quick eye to see the ruby crown, which the male flashes when he is excited. The female weaves an unusually intricate nest and fastens colorful lichens and mosses to the exterior with spiderwebs. Often builds the nest high in a mature tree, where it hangs from a branch that has overlapping leaves. "Kinglet" originates from the word *king,* referring to the male's red crown, and the diminutive suffix *let,* meaning "small."

YEAR-ROUND

Golden-crowned Kinglet
Regulus satrapa

Size: 4" (10 cm)

Male: Tiny, plump green-to-gray bird. Distinctive yellow-and-orange patch with a black border on the crown (top inset). White eyebrow mark. 2 white wing bars.

Female: same as male, but has a yellow crown with a black border, lacks any orange (bottom inset)

Juvenile: same as adults, but lacks gold on crown

Nest: pendulous; female builds; 1–2 broods per year

Eggs: 5–9; white or creamy with brown markings

Incubation: 14–15 days; female incubates

Fledging: 14–19 days; female and male feed the young

Migration: complete, to southern states, Mexico, and Central America; non-migrator in Maine

Food: insects, fruit, tree sap

Compare: Similar to the Ruby-crowned Kinglet (p. 211), but the Golden-crowned has an obvious crown. Female American Goldfinch (p. 305) is larger and has an all-black forehead.

Stan's Notes: Common year-round resident in the state, but might be more frequently seen during migration when flocks from farther north move through Maine. While most migrate south, some stay and are commonly seen in winter. Often seen in flocks with chickadees, nuthatches, woodpeckers, Brown Creepers, and Ruby-crowned Kinglets. Flicks its wings when moving around. Constructs an unusual hanging nest, often with moss, lichens, and spiderwebs, and lines it with bark and feathers. Can have so many eggs in its small nest that eggs are in two layers. Drinks tree sap and feeds by gleaning insects from trees. Can be very tame and approachable.

Red-breasted Nuthatch
Sitta canadensis

YEAR-ROUND

Size: 4½" (11 cm)

Male: Gray-backed bird with an obvious black eye line and black cap. Rust-red breast and belly.

Female: duller than male and has a gray cap and pale undersides

Juvenile: same as female

Nest: cavity; male and female excavate a cavity or move into a vacant hole; 1 brood per year

Eggs: 5–6; white with red-brown markings

Incubation: 11–12 days; female incubates

Fledging: 14–20 days; female and male feed the young

Migration: non-migrator to irruptive; moves around in search of food

Food: insects, insect eggs, seeds; comes to seed and suet feeders

Compare: The White-breasted Nuthatch (p. 219) is larger and has a white breast. Look for the rust-red breast and black eye line to help identify the Red-breasted Nuthatch.

Stan's Notes: The nuthatch climbs down trunks of trees headfirst, searching for insects. Like a chickadee, it grabs a seed from a feeder and flies off to crack it open. Wedges the seed into a crevice and pounds it open with several sharp blows. The name "Nuthatch" comes from the Middle English moniker *nuthak*, referring to the habit of hacking seeds open. Look for it in mature conifers, where it extracts seeds from pine cones. Excavates a cavity or takes an old woodpecker hole or a natural cavity and builds a nest within. Gives a series of nasal "yank-yank-yank" calls.

Black-capped Chickadee

Poecile atricapillus

YEAR-ROUND

Size: 5" (13 cm)

Male: Familiar gray bird with a black cap and throat patch. Tan sides and belly. White chest. Small white wing marks.

Female: same as male

Juvenile: same as adults

Nest: cavity; female and male excavate or use a nest box; 1 brood per year

Eggs: 5–9; white with fine brown markings

Incubation: 11–13 days; female and male incubate

Fledging: 14–18 days; female and male feed the young

Migration: non-migrator

Food: seeds, insects, fruit; will come to seed and suet feeders

Compare: The Tufted Titmouse (p. 225) is larger and has a crest.

Stan's Notes: Widespread, common bird throughout Maine. A perky backyard bird that can be attracted with a nest box or bird feeder. Usually the first to find a new seed or suet feeder. Can be tamed and hand-fed. Much of the diet comes from feeders, so it can be a common urban bird. Needs to feed every day in winter; forages even during the worst winter storms. Typically seen with nuthatches, woodpeckers, and other birds. Builds nest mostly with green moss, lined with fur. Named for its familiar "chika-dee-dee-dee-dee" call. Also gives a high-pitched, two-toned "fee-bee" call. Can have different calls in different regions.

White-breasted Nuthatch
Sitta carolinensis

YEAR-ROUND

Size: 5–6" (13–15 cm)

Male: Slate gray with a white face, breast and belly. Large white patch on the rump. Black cap and nape. Bill is long and thin, slightly upturned. Chestnut undertail.

Female: similar to male, but has a gray cap and nape

Juvenile: similar to female

Nest: cavity; female builds nest, with male's help; 1 brood per year

Eggs: 5–7; white with brown markings

Incubation: 11–12 days; female incubates

Fledging: 13–14 days; female and male feed the young

Migration: non-migrator

Food: insects, insect eggs, seeds; comes to seed and suet feeders

Compare: The Red-breasted Nuthatch (p. 215) is smaller and has a rust-red belly and distinctive black eye line. Look for the white breast to help identify the White-breasted Nuthatch.

Stan's Notes: The nuthatch hops headfirst down trees, looking for insects missed by birds climbing up. Its climbing agility is due to an extra-long hind toe claw, or nail, that is nearly twice the size of its front claws. "Nuthatch," from the Middle English *nuthak*, refers to the bird's habit of wedging a seed in a crevice and hacking it open. Often seen in flocks with chickadees, Brown Creepers, and Downy Woodpeckers. Mates stay together year-round, defending a small territory. Gives a characteristic "whi-whi-whi-whi" spring call during February and March. Abundant throughout Maine.

male

female

first
winter

Yellow-rumped Warbler
Setophaga coronata

SUMMER

Size: 5–6" (13–15 cm)

Male: Slate gray with black streaking on the chest. Yellow patches on the head, flanks, and rump. White chin and belly. 2 white wing bars.

Female: duller gray than the male, mixed with brown

Juvenile: first winter is similar to the adult female

Nest: cup; female builds; 2 broods per year

Eggs: 4–5; white with brown markings

Incubation: 12–13 days; female incubates

Fledging: 10–12 days; female and male feed the young

Migration: complete, to southern states, Mexico, and Central America

Food: insects, berries; visits suet feeders in spring

Compare: The Magnolia Warbler (p. 311) has more yellow. Male Yellow Warbler (p. 313) is all yellow with orange streaks on the breast. Palm Warbler (p. 315) has a yellow throat and chestnut crown. The male Common Yellowthroat (p. 307) has a yellow breast and distinctive black mask.

Stan's Notes: One of our most common warblers. Seems to prefer deciduous woods and forest edges but may be seen in any habitat during migration. Familiar call is a single robust "chip," heard mostly during migration and winter. Sings a wonderful song in spring. Comes to suet feeders in spring, when insect populations are low. Flits around the upper branches of tall trees. In the fall, the male molts to a dull color similar to the female, but he retains his yellow patches all year. Also called Myrtle Warbler. Sometimes called Butter-butt due to the yellow patch on its rump.

female
p. 115

male

Dark-eyed Junco
Junco hyemalis

YEAR-ROUND

Size: 5½" (14 cm)

Male: Plump, dark-eyed bird with a slate-gray to charcoal chest, head and back. White belly. Pink bill. White outer tail feathers appear like a white V in flight.

Female: round with brown plumage

Juvenile: similar to female, with streaking on the breast and head

Nest: cup; female builds nest, with male's help; 2 broods per year

Eggs: 3–5; white with reddish-brown markings

Incubation: 12–13 days; female incubates

Fledging: 10–13 days; male and female feed the young

Migration: complete, across the U.S.; non-migrator in Maine

Food: seeds, insects; visits ground and seed feeders

Compare: Rarely confused with any other bird. Look for the pink bill and small flocks feeding under feeders to identify the male Dark-eyed Junco.

Stan's Notes: One of Maine's most common winter birds. Migrates from Canada to Maine and beyond. Adheres to a rigid social hierarchy, with dominant birds chasing the less dominant ones. Look for the white outer tail feathers flashing in flight. Often seen in small flocks on the ground, where it uses its feet to simultaneously "double-scratch" to expose seeds and insects. Eats many weed seeds. Nests in a wide variety of wooded habitats. Several subspecies of Dark-eyed Junco were previously considered to be separate species. Males don't go as far south as females in winter.

Tufted Titmouse
Baeolophus bicolor

YEAR-ROUND

Size: 6" (15 cm)

Male: Slate gray with a white chest and belly. Pointed crest. Rust-brown wash on the flanks. Gray legs and dark eyes.

Female: same as male

Juvenile: same as adults

Nest: cavity; female lines an old woodpecker cavity; 2 broods per year

Eggs: 5–7; white with brown markings

Incubation: 13–14 days; female incubates

Fledging: 15–18 days; female and male feed the young

Migration: non-migrator; moves around in winter

Food: insects, seeds, fruit; will come to seed and suet feeders

Compare: The Black-capped Chickadee (p. 217) is a close relative but is smaller and lacks a crest. The White-breasted Nuthatch (p. 219) has a rust-brown undertail. Look for the pointed crest to help identify the Tufted Titmouse.

Stan's Notes: A common feeder bird that can be attracted with an offering of black oil sunflower seeds or suet. Can also be attracted with a nest box. Well known for its "peter-peter-peter" call, which it quickly repeats. Notorious for pulling hair from sleeping dogs, cats, and squirrels to line its nest. Usually seen only one or two at a time. Male feeds female during courtship and nesting. The prefix *tit* in the common name comes from a Scandinavian word meaning "little." Suffix *mouse* is derived from the Old English word *mase*, meaning "bird." Simply translated, it is a "small bird."

Eastern Phoebe
Sayornis phoebe

SUMMER

Size: 7" (18 cm)

Male: Plain gray with slightly darker wings and a light-olive belly. Thin, dark bill.

Female: same as male

Juvenile: same as adults

Nest: cup; female builds; 2 broods per year

Eggs: 4–5; white without markings

Incubation: 15–16 days; female incubates

Fledging: 15–16 days; male and female feed the young

Migration: complete, to southern states and Mexico

Food: insects

Compare: The Gray Catbird (p. 235) has a black crown and a chestnut patch under its tail. The Eastern Phoebe lacks any distinctive markings. Listen for its well-enunciated "fee-bee" call and look for the hawking and tail-pumping behaviors to help identify this bird.

Stan's Notes: A sparrow-size bird that often perches on the end of a dead branch. Found in forests, yards, and farms. In a process called hawking, it waits for a passing insect. When a bug flies near, it launches out to catch it and then returns to the same branch, a process called hawking. It has a distinctive habit of pumping its tail up and down while perching. Builds nest beneath the eaves of houses, under bridges, or in other sheltered spots. Uses mud, grass, and moss for nest materials and hair (and sometimes feathers) for the lining. The common name is derived from its distinct "fee-bee" call, which it repeats over and over from the top of dead branches.

Eastern Kingbird
Tyrannus tyrannus

SUMMER

Size: 8" (20 cm)

Male: Mostly gray and black with a white chin and belly. Black head and tail with a distinct white band on the tip of the tail. Concealed red crown, rarely seen.

Female: same as male

Juvenile: same as adults

Nest: cup; female builds; 1 brood per year

Eggs: 3–4; white with brown markings

Incubation: 16–18 days; female incubates

Fledging: 16–18 days; female and male feed the young

Migration: complete, to Mexico, Central America, and South America

Food: insects, fruit

Compare: The American Robin (p. 239) is larger and has a rust-red breast. The Eastern Phoebe (p. 227) is smaller and has an olive-green belly. Look for the white tail band to identify the Kingbird.

Stan's Notes: A summer resident in open fields and prairies. As many as 20 birds migrate in a group. Returns to the mating ground in spring, where pairs defend their territory. Seems to be unafraid of other birds and chases larger birds. Given the common name "King" for its bold attitude and behavior. In a hunting technique known as hawking, it perches on a branch and watches for insects, flies out to catch one, and then returns to the same perch. Swoops from perch to perch when hunting. Becomes very vocal during late summer, when family members call back and forth to one another while hunting for insects. In strong wind, it will fly into the wind, stalling its flight and appearing hover when hunting for insects.

Great Crested Flycatcher
Myiarchus crinitus

SUMMER

Size: 8" (20 cm)

Male: Gray head with a prominent crest. Gray back and throat. Yellow from the belly to the base of a reddish-brown tail. Lower bill is yellow at the base.

Female: same as male

Juvenile: same as adults

Nest: cavity; female and male stuff a vacant woodpecker cavity or nest box; 1 brood per year

Eggs: 4–6; white to buff with brown markings

Incubation: 13–15 days; female incubates

Fledging: 14–21 days; female and male feed the young

Migration: complete, to Mexico and Central America

Food: insects, fruit

Compare: The Eastern Kingbird (p. 229) has a white band across its tail. The Eastern Phoebe (p. 227) is similar, but it lacks a crest and yellow belly. Look for the crest to identify the Flycatcher.

Stan's Notes: A common bird of wooded areas throughout the state. It lives high up in trees, rarely coming to the ground. Makes long flights from treetop to treetop, moving from one hunting area to another. Gleans insects from tree leaves. Often heard before seen. "Great Crested" refers to the set of extra-long feathers on top of its head (crest), which the bird raises when alert or agitated, like the Northern Cardinal. Nests in an old woodpecker hole but can be attracted with a man-made nest box that has an entrance hole 1½–2½ inches (4–6 cm) in diameter. Often stuffs the cavity with a collection of fur, feathers, string, and snake skins.

male
p. 287

female

Pine Grosbeak
Pinicola enucleator

YEAR-ROUND WINTER

Size: 9" (23 cm)

Female: Plump gray finch with a long dark tail. Dark wings with two white wing bars. Head and rump have a dull-yellow tinge. Short, pointed dark bill.

Male: plump bird, overall rose-red and gray

Juvenile: female is similar to the adult female; male has a touch of red on the head and rump

Nest: cup; female builds; 1 brood per year

Eggs: 4–5; green with small, dark markings

Incubation: 13–15 days; female incubates

Fledging: 13–20 days; female and male feed the young

Migration: non-migrator to irruptive; moves around in winter to find food

Food: seeds, fruit, insects; will come to seed feeders

Compare: The female Evening Grosbeak (p. 323) is slightly smaller and lacks the dull-yellow head of the female Pine Grosbeak.

Stan's Notes: This winter finch is common in Maine in some years and not so common in others. A very tame and approachable seed eater. Often seen along roads or on the ground, eating tiny grains of sand and dirt, which help aid digestion. Favors coniferous woods, rarely moving out of coniferous regions during summer, but also likes mixed forests. Will bathe in fluffy snow. Flies in a typical finch-like undulating pattern while giving soft, whistle "cheer" calls. Male sings a rich, beautiful song all year long. Male and female develop a pouch in the bottom of their mouths (buccal pouch) during the breeding season for transporting seeds to their young.

Gray Catbird
Dumetella carolinensis

SUMMER

Size: 9" (23 cm)

Male: Handsome slate-gray bird with a black crown and a long, thin black bill. Often lifts up its tail, exposing a chestnut patch beneath.

Female: same as male

Juvenile: same as adults

Nest: cup; female and male build; 2 broods per year

Eggs: 4–6; blue-green without markings

Incubation: 12–13 days; female incubates

Fledging: 10–11 days; female and male feed the young

Migration: complete, to southern states

Food: insects, occasional fruit; visits suet feeders

Compare: The Eastern Phoebe (p. 227) is smaller and has an olive belly. The Eastern Kingbird (p. 229) is similar in size but has a white belly and a white band across its tail. To identify the Gray Catbird, look for the black crown and chestnut patch under the tail.

Stan's Notes: Returns to Maine by the last week in April. A secretive bird, more often heard than seen. The Chippewa Indians gave it a name that means "the bird that cries with grief" due to its raspy call. Called "Catbird" because the sound is like the meowing of a house cat. Often mimics other birds, rarely repeating the same phrases. Found in forest edges, backyards, and parks. Builds its nest with small twigs. Nests in thick shrubs and quickly flies back into shrubs if approached. If a cowbird lays an egg in its nest, the catbird will quickly break it and eject it.

male
p. 33

female

Rusty Blackbird
Euphagus carolinus

SUMMER
MIGRATION

Size: 9" (22.5 cm)

Male: Overall gray bird. Rusty edges of feathers. Yellow eyes. Has a short, pointed thin bill. Non-breeding is much browner with a gray rump and black patch around each eye.

Female: glossy black in color with highlights of blue and purple, bright yellow eyes, has a short, pointed thin bill, non-breeding plumage is more of a rusty brown than glossy black

Juvenile: similar to female

Nest: cup; female builds; 1–2 broods per year

Eggs: 4–5; bluish with brown markings

Incubation: 12–14 days; female incubates

Fledging: 11–13 days; female and male feed the young

Migration: complete, to southeastern states

Food: insects, seeds

Compare: The female Red-winged Blackbird (p. 149) is slightly smaller and heavily streaked, with prominent white eyebrows. The female Brown-headed Cowbird (p. 137) is uniform light brown in color, with dark eyes. Smaller than the Common Grackle (p. 35), which has a longer tail.

Stan's Notes: This bird nests across the northern half of Maine in small loose colonies, often preferring more wooded, swampy areas. Male feeds female while she incubates. Gathers in large groups and with other blackbirds to migrate each fall. When in flight, end of tail often appears squared.

male

female

American Robin
Turdus migratorius

YEAR-ROUND
SUMMER

Size: 9–11" (23–28 cm)

Male: Familiar gray bird with a dark rust-red breast and a nearly black head and tail. White chin with black streaks. White eye-ring.

Female: similar to male, with a duller rust-red breast and a gray head

Juvenile: similar to female, with a speckled breast and brown back

Nest: cup; female builds with help from the male; 2–3 broods per year

Eggs: 4–7; pale blue without markings

Incubation: 12–14 days; female incubates

Fledging: 14–16 days; female and male feed the young

Migration: complete, to southern states; non-migrator in southern half of Maine; moves around to find food in winter

Food: insects, fruit, berries, earthworms

Compare: Familiar bird to all. To differentiate the male from the female, compare the nearly black head and rust-red chest of the male with the gray head and duller chest of the female.

Stan's Notes: Some will not migrate, spending the winter in low swampy areas, feeding on leftover berries and insect eggs. Can be heard singing all night in spring. City robins sing louder than country robins in order to hear one another over traffic and noise. A robin isn't listening for worms when it turns its head to one side. It is focusing its sight out of one eye to look for dirt moving, which is caused by worms moving. Territorial, often fighting its reflection in a window. Males have dark heads and a brighter red breast than females. In winter, it switches its diet from insects to fruit.

Northern Shrike
Lanius borealis

WINTER

Size: 10" (25 cm)

Male: Overall gray bird with black wings and tail. Distinctive black mask across eyes. A small white patch on black wings, seen in flight. Large black bill with a hooked tip.

Female: same as male

Juvenile: tan to light brown overall with dark wings, finely streaked chest

Nest: cup; female and male construct; 1 brood per year

Eggs: 4–6; gray to olive-green with brown markings

Incubation: 15–16 days; female incubates

Fledging: 18–20 days; female and male feed the young

Migration: complete, to Maine

Food: large insects, small mammals, small birds

Compare: The Canada Jay (p. 245) is larger and lacks the black mask and wings. Look for the black mask and large black bill with a hooked tip to help identify the Northern Shrike.

Stan's Notes: Songbird that acts like a bird of prey. Often seen out in the open, where it sits still for long periods of time watching for prey movement. Unlike a bird of prey, its feet aren't strong enough to hold prey still while it eats. Skewers large insects, mice, and other prey on barbed wire fences, long thorns, or other sharp objects to hold prey still while tearing it apart. For this reason, it is also called Butcher Bird. Winter populations and migratory behavior may be influenced by the availability of food.

displaying

Northern Mockingbird
Mimus polyglottos

YEAR-ROUND
MIGRATION

Size: 10" (25 cm)

Male: Silvery-gray head and back with a light-gray breast and belly. White wing patches, seen in flight or during display. Tail mostly black with white outer tail feathers. Black bill.

Female: same as male

Juvenile: dull gray with a heavily streaked breast and a gray bill

Nest: cup; female and male construct; 2 broods per year, sometimes more

Eggs: 3–5; blue-green with brown markings

Incubation: 12–13 days; female incubates

Fledging: 11–13 days; female and male feed the young

Migration: partial to non-migrator in Maine; moves around to find food

Food: insects, fruit

Compare: The Gray Catbird (p. 235) is slate gray and lacks wing patches. Look for the Mockingbird to spread its wings, flash its white wing patches, and wag its tail from side to side.

Stan's Notes: A very animated bird. Performs an elaborate mating dance. Facing each other with heads and tails erect, pairs will run toward each other, flashing their white wing patches, and then retreat to cover nearby. Thought to flash the wing patches to scare up insects when hunting. Sits for long periods on top of shrubs. Imitates other birds (vocal mimicry); hence the common name. Young males often sing at night. Often unafraid of people, allowing for close observation.

Canada Jay
Perisoreus canadensis

YEAR-ROUND

Size: 11½" (29 cm)

Male: Large gray bird with a black nape and white chest. White patch on forehead. Short black bill and dark eyes.

Female: same as male

Juvenile: soot-gray plumage with a faint white whisker mark on each side of the face

Nest: cup; male and female build; 1 brood per year

Eggs: 3–4; grayish white with fine markings or may be unmarked

Incubation: 16–18 days; female incubates

Fledging: 14–15 days; male and female feed the young

Migration: non-migrator

Food: insects, seeds, fruit, nuts; visits seed feeders

Compare: Blue Jay (p. 93) has a similar size, but it has a crest and blue coloring. Look for the white forehead to help identify the Canada Jay.

Stan's Notes: A bird of northern woods. Likes evergreen forests, mixed woods, and campsites. Travels around in small family units of 3–5 birds, making good company for campers. Reminds some people of an overgrown chickadee. Also called Camp Robber because it rummages through camps, looking for scraps of food. Also known as Gray Jay or Whiskey Jack. Easily tamed, it will fly to your hand if offered raisins or nuts. Will eat just about anything. Stores extra food for the winter, balling it together in a sticky mass, and then placing it on a tree branch, often concealing it with lichen or bark. Doesn't vocalize much but will give a variety of chatters and whistles.

Eurasian Collared-Dove
Streptopelia decaocto

YEAR-ROUND

Size: 12½" (32 cm)

Male: Head, neck, breast, and belly are gray to tan. Back, wings, and tail are slightly darker. Thin black collar with a white border on the nape of the neck. Tail is long and squared.

Female: same as male

Juvenile: similar to adults

Nest: platform; female and male build; 2–3 broods per year

Eggs: 3–5; cream-white without markings

Incubation: 12–14 days; female and male incubate

Fledging: 12–14 days; female and male feed the young

Migration: non-migrator; moves around to find food

Food: seeds; will visit ground and seed feeders

Compare: The Mourning Dove (p. 163) is slightly smaller and darker. The Rock Pigeon (p. 249) has colorful iridescent patches. Look for the black collar on the nape and the squared tail to help identify the Eurasian Collared-Dove.

Stan's Notes: A non-native bird. Moved into the US in the 1980s after inadvertent introduction to the Bahamas; reached Maine in the early 2000s. It has been expanding its range across North America and is predicted to spread just like it did through Europe from Asia. Unknown how this "new" bird will affect populations of the native Mourning Dove. Nearly identical to the Ringed Turtle-Dove, a common pet bird. The dark mark on the back of the neck gave rise to the common name. Look for flashes of white in the tail and dark wing tips when it lands or takes off.

Rock Pigeon
Columba livia

YEAR-ROUND

Size: 13" (33 cm)

Male: No set color pattern. Shades of gray to white with patches of gleaming, iridescent green and blue. Often has a light rump patch.

Female: same as male

Juvenile: same as adults

Nest: platform; female builds; 3–4 broods per year

Eggs: 1–2; white without markings

Incubation: 18–20 days; female and male incubate

Fledging: 25–26 days; female and male feed the young

Migration: non-migrator

Food: seeds, fruit; visits ground and seed feeders

Compare: The Eurasian Collared-Dove (p. 247) has a black collar on the nape. The Mourning Dove (p. 163) is smaller and light brown and lacks the variety of color combinations of the Rock Pigeon.

Stan's Notes: Also known as the Domestic Pigeon. Formerly known as the Rock Dove. Introduced to North America from Europe by the early settlers. Most common around cities and barnyards, where it scratches for seeds. One of the few birds with a wide variety of colors, produced by years of selective breeding while in captivity. Parents feed the young a regurgitated liquid known as crop-milk for the first few days of life. One of the few birds that can drink without tilting its head back. Nests under bridges or on buildings, balconies, barns, and sheds. Was once thought to be a nuisance in cities and was poisoned. Now, many cities have Peregrine Falcons feeding on Rock Pigeons, which keeps their numbers in check.

soaring

juvenile

Sharp-shinned Hawk

Accipiter striatus

**YEAR-ROUND
SUMMER**

Size: 10–14" (25–36 cm); up to 2' wingspan

Male: Small woodland hawk with a gray back and head and a rust-red chest. Short wings. Long, squared tail and several dark tail bands, with the widest at the end of the tail. Red eyes.

Female: same as male but larger

Juvenile: same size as adults, with a brown back, heavy streaking on the chest and yellow eyes

Nest: platform; female builds; 1 brood per year

Eggs: 4–5; white with brown markings

Incubation: 32–35 days; female incubates

Fledging: 24–27 days; female and male feed the young

Migration: complete, to southern states, Mexico, Central America; non-migrator in most of Maine

Food: birds, small mammals

Compare: Cooper's Hawk (p. 255) is much larger and has a larger head, a slightly longer neck and a rounded tail. Red-shouldered Hawk (p. 183) is larger and lacks a gray back. Look for the squared tail to help identify the Sharp-shinned Hawk.

Stan's Notes: A common hawk of backyards, parks, and woodlands. Constructs its nest with sticks, usually high in a tree. Typically seen swooping in on birds visiting feeders and chasing them as they flee. Its short wingspan and long tail help it to maneuver through thick stands of trees in pursuit of prey. Calls a loud, high-pitched "kik-kik-kik-kik." Named "Sharp-shinned" for the sharp projection (keel) on the leading edge of its shin. A bird's shin is actually below the ankle (rather than above it, like ours) on the tarsus bone of its foot. In most birds, the tarsus bone is rounded, not sharp.

breeding
p. 171

displaying

winter

Willet
Tringa semipalmatus

SUMMER

Size: 14–16" (36–40 cm)

Male: Winter plumage is gray with a white belly. A distinctive black-and-white wing lining pattern, seen in flight or during display. Gray bill and legs.

Female: same as male

Juvenile: similar to breeding adult, more tan in color

Nest: ground; female builds; 1 brood per year

Eggs: 3–5; olive-green with dark markings

Incubation: 24–28 days; male and female incubate

Fledging: 1–2 days; female and male feed young

Migration: complete, to southern coastal states, coastal Central and South America

Food: insects, small fish, crabs, worms, clams

Compare: Greater Yellowlegs (p. 169) is slightly smaller and has a longer neck and yellow legs. Killdeer (p. 157) has 2 black bands on the neck.

Stan's Notes: A common summer coastal resident. One of the few shorebirds that is seen away from water, sometimes standing on fence posts. It appears a rich, warm brown during the breeding season and rather plain gray during the winter, but it always has a striking black-and-white wing pattern when seen in flight. Uses its black-and-white wing patches to display to its mate. Named after the "pill-will-willet" call it gives during the breeding season. Gives a "kip-kip-kip" alarm call when it takes flight. Nests along the Gulf and East Coasts, in some western states and Canada.

soaring

juvenile

Cooper's Hawk
Accipiter cooperii

Size: 14–20" (36–51 cm); up to 3' wingspan

Male: Medium-size hawk with short wings and a long, rounded tail with several black bands. Slate-gray back, rusty breast, dark wing tips. Gray bill with a bright-yellow spot at the base. Dark-red eyes.

Female: similar to male but larger

Juvenile: brown back, brown streaking on the breast, bright-yellow eyes

Nest: platform; male selects nest site and does most of the nest construction with female's help; 1 brood per year

Eggs: 4; light blue to nearly white without markings

Incubation: 32–36 days; female and male incubate

Fledging: 28–32 days; male and female feed the young

Migration: complete, to southern states; non-migrator in southern edge of Maine

Food: small birds, mammals

Compare: The Sharp-shinned Hawk (p. 251) is much smaller and lighter gray and has a squared tail. Look for the banded, rounded tail to help identify Cooper's Hawk.

YEAR-ROUND
SUMMER

Stan's Notes: A common year-round resident hawk of woodlands. Stubby wings help it to navigate around trees while it chases small birds. Will ambush prey, flying into heavy brush or even running on the ground in pursuit. Comes to feeders, hunting for birds. Flies with long glides followed by a few quick flaps. Calls a loud, clear "cack-cack-cack-cack." The young have gray eyes that turn bright yellow at 1 year and turn dark red later, after 3–5 years.

juvenile

in-flight
juvenile

in flight

Peregrine Falcon
Falco peregrinus

SUMMER MIGRATION

Size: 16–20" (41–51 cm); up to 3¾' wingspan

Male: Dark-gray back, dark "hood" head marking, wide black mustache and tan-to-white chest. Horizontal bars on belly, legs, and undertail. Yellow base of bill, eye-ring, and legs.

Female: similar to male but noticeably larger

Juvenile: overall darker than adults, with heavy streaking on the chest and belly

Nest: ground (scrape) on a cliff edge, tall building, bridge or smokestack; 1 brood per year

Eggs: 3–4; white, some with brown markings

Incubation: 29–32 days; female and male incubate

Fledging: 35–42 days; male and female feed the young

Migration: complete to partial migrator; moves around to find food in winter; most move out of Maine

Food: birds (Rock Pigeons in cities, shorebirds and waterfowl in rural areas)

Compare: The American Kestrel (p. 155) is smaller and has 2 vertical black stripes on its face. Look for the dark "hood" head marking and mustache marks to identify the Peregrine Falcon.

Stan's Notes: A wide-bodied raptor that hunts many bird species. The larger females hunt larger prey. Lives in many cities, diving (stooping) on pigeons at speeds of up to 200 mph (322 kph), which knocks them to the ground. Soars with its wings flat, often riding thermals. During courtship, the male brings food to the female and performs aerial displays. Likes to nest on a high ledge or platform for a good view of its territory. A solitary nester and monogamous.

female
p. 195

male

soaring

SUMMER

Northern Harrier
Circus hudsonius

Size: 18–22" (45–56 cm); up to 4' wingspan

Male: Slender, low-flying hawk. Silver-gray with a large white rump patch and white belly. Long tail with faint narrow bands. Black wing tips. Yellow eyes.

Female: dark brown back, brown streaking on breast and belly, large white rump patch, thin black tail bands, black wing tips, yellow eyes

Juvenile: similar to female, with an orange chest

Nest: ground; female and male construct; 1 brood per year

Eggs: 4–8; bluish white without markings

Incubation: 31–32 days; female incubates

Fledging: 30–35 days; male and female feed the young

Migration: complete, to southern states, Mexico, and Central America; winters in coastal Maine

Food: mice, snakes, insects, small birds

Compare: Slimmer than Red-tailed Hawk (p. 199). Cooper's Hawk (p. 255) has a rusty breast. Look for a low-gliding hawk with a large white rump patch to identify the male Harrier.

Stan's Notes: One of the easiest of hawks to identify. Glides just above the ground, following the contours of the land while searching for prey. Holds its wings just above horizontal, tilting back and forth in the wind, similar to Turkey Vultures. Formerly called the Marsh Hawk due to its habit of hunting over marshes. Feeds and nests on the ground. Will also preen and rest on the ground. Unlike other hawks, mainly uses its hearing to find prey, followed by sight. At any age, has a distinctive owl-like face disk.

in flight

Canada Goose
Branta canadensis

YEAR-ROUND
SUMMER

Size: 25–43" (64–109 cm); up to 5½' wingspan

Male: Large gray goose with a black neck and head. White chin and cheek strap.

Female: same as male

Juvenile: same as adults

Nest: platform on the ground; female constructs; 1 brood per year

Eggs: 5–10; white without markings

Incubation: 25–30 days; female incubates

Fledging: 42–55 days; male and female teach the young to feed

Migration: non-migrator to partial migrator; moves around to find open water in winter

Food: aquatic plants, insects, seeds

Compare: Large goose that is rarely confused with any other bird.

Stan's Notes: Formerly killed off (extirpated) in many areas, it was reintroduced and is now a common year-round resident. Adapting to our changed environment very well, it now breeds in Maine. Calls a classic "honk-honk-honk," especially in flight. Flocks fly in a large V when traveling long distances. Begins breeding in the second or third year. Adults mate for many years. If threatened, they will hiss as a warning. Males stand as sentinels at the edge of their group and will bob their heads and become aggressive if approached. Adults molt their primary flight feathers while raising their young, rendering family groups temporarily flightless. Several subspecies vary in the U.S. Generally eastern groups are paler than western. Their size also varies, decreasing northward. The smallest subspecies is in the Arctic.

in flight

Great Blue Heron
Ardea herodias

YEAR-ROUND
SUMMER

Size: 42–48" (107–122 cm); up to 6' wingspan

Male: Tall and gray. Black eyebrows end in long plumes at the back of the head. Long yellow bill. Long feathers at the base of the neck drop down in a kind of necklace. Long legs.

Female: same as male

Juvenile: same as adults, but more brown than gray, with a black crown; lacks plumes

Nest: platform in a colony; male and female build; 1 brood per year

Eggs: 3–5; blue-green without markings

Incubation: 27–28 days; female and male incubate

Fledging: 56–60 days; male and female feed the young

Migration: complete, to southern states, Mexico, and Central and South America

Food: small fish, frogs, insects, snakes, baby birds

Compare: Great Egret (p. 303) is similar in shape, but it is smaller and all white. Look for the long, yellow bill to help identify the Great Blue Heron.

Stan's Notes: One of the most common herons. Found in open water, from small ponds to large lakes. Stalks small fish in shallow water. Will strike at mice, squirrels, and nearly anything it comes across. In flight, it holds its neck in an S shape and slightly cups its wings, while the legs trail straight out behind. Nests in a colony of up to 100 birds. Nests in trees near or hanging over water. Barks like a dog when startled. Most common along the coast.

male

female

Ruby-throated Hummingbird

Archilochus colubris

SUMMER

Size: 3–3½" (7.5–9 cm)

Male: Tiny, iridescent green bird. Black throat patch reflects bright ruby red in direct sunlight.

Female: same as male but lacks a throat patch

Juvenile: same as female

Nest: cup; female builds; 1–2 broods per year

Eggs: 2; white without markings

Incubation: 12–14 days; female incubates

Fledging: 14–18 days; female feeds the young

Migration: complete, to southern states, Mexico, and Central America

Food: nectar, insects; will come to nectar feeders

Compare: No other bird is as tiny. The Sphinx Moth also hovers at flowers, but it has clear wings, doesn't hum in flight, moves much slower than the Ruby-throated and can be approached.

Stan's Notes: This is the smallest bird in the state. Can fly straight up, straight down, or backward and hover in midair. Does not sing but chatters or buzzes to communicate. Weighs about the same as a U.S. penny; it takes about five average-size hummingbirds to equal the weight of one chickadee. The wings create the humming sound. Flaps 50–60 times or more per second when flying at top speed. Breathes 250 times per minute. Heart beats up to 1,260 times per minute. Builds a stretchy nest with plant material and spiderwebs, gluing pieces of lichen to the exterior for camouflage. Attracted to colorful, tubular flowers. Will extract and eat insects trapped in spiderwebs. A long-distance migrator, wintering as far south as the tropics of Central America.

female
p. 191

male

Wood Duck
Aix sponsa

SUMMER

Size: 17–20" (43–51 cm)

Male: Small, highly ornamented dabbling duck. Mostly green head and crest patterned with black and white. Rusty chest and a white belly. Red eyes.

Female: brown duck with a bright-white eye-ring, not-so-obvious crest and blue patch on wings (speculum), often hidden

Juvenile: similar to female

Nest: cavity; female lines an old woodpecker cavity or a nest box in a tree; 1–2 brood per year

Eggs: 10–15; cream-white without markings

Incubation: 28–36 days; female incubates

Fledging: 56–68 days; female teaches the young to feed

Migration: complete, to southern states

Food: aquatic insects, plants, seeds

Compare: More colorful than the male Green-winged Teal (p. 173). Male Hooded Merganser (p. 69) is similar in size, but has a crest "hood."

Stan's Notes: A common duck of quiet, shallow backwater ponds. Nearly went extinct around 1900 due to overhunting, but it's doing well now. Nests in a tree cavity or a nest box in a tree. Seen flying in forests or perching on high branches. Female takes off with a loud squealing call and enters the nest cavity from full flight. Lays some eggs in a neighboring nest (egg dumping), resulting in more than 20 eggs in some clutches. Hatchlings stay in the nest for 24 hours, then jump from as high as 60 feet (18 m) to the ground or water to follow their mother. They never return to the nest.

female
p. 197

male

Mallard

Anas platyrhynchos

YEAR-ROUND
SUMMER

Size: 19–21" (48–53 cm)

Male: Large, bulbous green head, white necklace, and rust-brown or chestnut chest. Gray-and-white sides. Yellow bill. Orange legs and feet.

Female: brown with an orange-and-black bill and blue-and-white wing mark (speculum)

Juvenile: same as female but with a yellow bill

Nest: ground; female builds; 1 brood per year

Eggs: 7–10; greenish to whitish, unmarked

Incubation: 26–30 days; female incubates

Fledging: 42–52 days; female leads the young to food

Migration: complete, to southern states; non-migrator in parts of Maine

Food: seeds, plants, aquatic insects; will come to ground feeders offering corn

Compare: Most people recognize this common duck. The male Red-breasted Merganser (p. 271) is smaller, lacking the Merganser's shaggy crest and large orange bill. Look for the green head and yellow bill to identify the male Mallard.

Stan's Notes: A familiar dabbling duck of lakes and ponds. Also found in rivers, streams, and some backyards. Tips forward to feed on vegetation on the bottom of shallow water. The name "Mallard" comes from the Latin word *masculus,* meaning "male," referring to the male's habit of taking no part in raising the young. Male and female have white underwings and white tails, but only the male has black central tail feathers that curl upward. Unlike the female, the male doesn't quack. Returns to its birthplace each year.

female
p. 207

male

Red-breasted Merganser
Mergus serrator

YEAR-ROUND
SUMMER
MIGRATION
WINTER

Size: 23" (58 cm)

Male: A shaggy green head and crest. Prominent white collar. Rusty breast. Black-and-white body. Long orange bill.

Female: overall brown to gray with a shaggy reddish head and crest, long orange bill

Juvenile: similar to female

Nest: ground; female builds; 1 brood per year

Eggs: 5–10; olive-green without markings

Incubation: 29–30 days; female incubates

Fledging: 55–65 days; female feeds young

Migration: complete, to coastal Maine, southern coastal states, Central America, and Mexico

Food: fish, aquatic insects

Compare: The male Hooded Merganser (p. 69) has a large white patch on the head, unlike the green head of male Red-breasted Merganser.

Stan's Notes: A winter resident of far southwestern Maine, commonly seen on the coast. This duck is a very fast flier, clocked at up to 100 miles (161 km) per hour. Frequently seen flying low across the water. Needs a long run for takeoff with wings flapping to get airborne. Serrated bill helps it catch slippery fish. Usually is a silent duck. Male sometimes gives a soft, catlike meow. Female gives a harsh "krrr-croak." Doesn't breed before 2 years of age. The male abandons the female just after eggs are laid. Females often share nests. Breeds across Alaska, northern Canada and inland Maine, wintering on the coast. The young leave the nest within 24 hours of hatching, never to return.

in flight

female
p. 289

male

Common Merganser
Mergus merganser

Size: 26–28" (66–71 cm)

Male: Long, thin, duck-like bird with a green head and black back. White sides, chest, and neck. Long, pointed, orange bill. Often looks black and white in poor light.

Female: same size and shape as the male, with a rust-red head and ragged "hair," gray body, white chest, and chin

Juvenile: same as female

Nest: cavity; female lines an old woodpecker hole or a natural cavity; 1 brood per year

Eggs: 9–11; ivory without markings

Incubation: 28–33 days; female incubates

Fledging: 70–80 days; female feeds the young

Migration: complete, to southern states and Mexico, to coast during winter

Food: small fish, aquatic insects, amphibians

Compare: The male Mallard (p. 269) is smaller and lacks the black back and long, pointed orange bill.

Stan's Notes: Seen on any open water during the winter usually near the coast. A large, shallow-water diver that feeds on fish in 10–15 feet (3–4.5 m) of water. Bill has a fine, serrated-like edge that helps catch slippery fish. Female often lays some eggs in other merganser nests (egg dumping), resulting in up to 15 young in some broods. Male leaves female once she starts incubating. Orphans are accepted by other merganser mothers with young. Fast flight, often low and close to the water, in groups but not in formation.

female
p. 309

male

American Redstart
Setophaga ruticilla

SUMMER

Size: 5" (13 cm)

Male: Striking black warbler with orange patches on the sides, wings, and tail. White belly.

Female: olive-brown with yellow patches on the sides, wings and tail, white belly

Juvenile: same as female; male attains orange tinges in the second year

Nest: cup; female builds; 1 brood per year

Eggs: 3–5; off-white with brown markings

Incubation: 12 days; female incubates

Fledging: 9 days; female and male feed the young

Migration: complete, to Mexico, Central America, and South America

Food: insects, seeds, occasionally berries

Compare: The male Baltimore Oriole (p. 277) and male Red-winged Blackbird (p. 31) are much larger. The male American Redstart is the only small black-and-orange bird flitting around the top of trees.

Stan's Notes: This is a common and widespread breeding warbler in Maine. Found in woodlands, parks, and yards and at forest edges. Prefers large, unbroken tracts of forest. Appears hyperactive when it feeds, hovering and darting back and forth to glean insects from leaves. Often droops wings and fans tail before launching out to catch an insect. Look for the flashing black-and-orange colors of the male high up in trees. First-year males have yellow markings and look like the females. Sings a high-pitched song that builds in intensity and then suddenly ends.

female
p. 321

male

Baltimore Oriole
Icterus galbula

SUMMER

Size: 7–8" (18–20 cm)

Male: Flaming orange with a black head and back. White-and-orange wing bars. Orange-and-black tail. Gray bill and dark eyes.

Female: pale yellow with orange tones, gray-brown wings, white wing bars, gray bill, dark eyes

Juvenile: same as female

Nest: pendulous; female builds; 1 brood per year

Eggs: 4–5; bluish with brown markings

Incubation: 12–14 days; female incubates

Fledging: 12–14 days; female and male feed the young

Migration: complete, to southern states, Mexico, Central America, and South America

Food: insects, fruit, nectar; comes to nectar, orange-half and grape-jelly feeders

Compare: The male American Redstart (p. 275) has much less orange. Look for the flaming orange to identify the male Baltimore Oriole.

Stan's Notes: A fantastic songster, often heard before seen. Easily attracted to a feeder that offers sugar water (nectar), orange halves, or grape jelly. Parents bring their young to feeders. Sits at the top of trees, feeding on caterpillars. Female builds a sock-like nest at the outermost branches of tall trees. Prefers parks, yards, and forests and often returns to the same area year after year. Seen during migration and summer. Some of the last birds to arrive in spring (May) and some of the first to leave in the fall (September). Young males turn orange-and-black at 1½ years of age.

male

female
p. 109

yellow
male

House Finch
Haemorhous mexicanus

YEAR-ROUND

Size: 5" (13 cm)

Male: Small finch with a red-to-orange face, throat, chest, and rump. Brown cap. Brown marking behind eyes. White belly with brown streaks. Brown wings with white streaks.

Female: brown with a heavily streaked white chest

Juvenile: similar to female

Nest: cup, occasionally in a cavity; female builds; 2 broods per year

Eggs: 4–5; pale blue, lightly marked

Incubation: 12–14 days; female incubates

Fledging: 15–19 days; female and male feed the young

Migration: non-migrator to partial; will move around to find food

Food: seeds, fruit, leaf buds; visits seed feeders and feeders that offer grape jelly

Compare: The male Purple Finch (p. 281) has a red cap. The male Pine Grosbeak (p. 287) is much larger. Look for the brown cap and streaked belly to help identify the male House Finch.

Stan's Notes: Can be a common bird at your feeders. Very social, visiting feeders in small flocks. Likes to nest in hanging flower baskets. Male sings a loud, cheerful warbling song. Incubating female is fed by the male. It was originally introduced to Long Island, New York, from the western U.S. in the 1940s and is now found throughout the country. Suffers from a disease that causes the eyes to crust, resulting in blindness and death. Rarely, males are yellow (inset), perhaps due to poor diet.

female
p. 121

male

Purple Finch
Haemorhous purpureus

YEAR-ROUND

Size: 6" (15 cm)

Male: Raspberry-red head, cap, chest, back, and rump. Brownish wings and tail. Large bill.

Female: heavily streaked brown-and-white bird with bold white eyebrows

Juvenile: same as female

Nest: cup; female and male build; 1 brood per year

Eggs: 4–5; greenish blue with brown markings

Incubation: 12–13 days; female incubates

Fledging: 13–14 days; female and male feed the young

Migration: non-migrator to irruptive; moves around in winter to find food

Food: seeds, insects, fruit; comes to seed feeders

Compare: The male House Finch (p. 279) has a brown cap and a streaked belly. Male Pine Grosbeak (p. 287) is much larger. Look for the raspberry cap to help identify the male Purple Finch.

Stan's Notes: A year-round resident throughout Maine. Travels in flocks of up to 50 birds. Visits seed feeders along with House Finches, which makes it hard to tell them apart. Feeds mainly on seeds; ash tree seeds are an important source of food. Found in coniferous forests, mixed woods, woodland edges, and suburban backyards. Flies in the typical undulating, up-and-down pattern of finches. Sings a rich, loud song. Gives a distinctive "tic" note only in flight. Male is not purple. The Latin species name *purpureus* means "purple" (or other reddish colors).

female
p. 319

male

Scarlet Tanager
Piranga olivacea

SUMMER

Size: 7" (18 cm)

Male: Bright scarlet with coal-black wings and tail. Ivory bill and dark eyes.

Female: drab greenish yellow with olive wings and tail, whitish wing linings and dark eyes

Juvenile: same as female

Nest: cup; female builds; 1 brood per year

Eggs: 4–5; blue-green with brown markings

Incubation: 13–14 days; female incubates

Fledging: 9–11 days; female and male feed the young

Migration: complete, to Central and South America

Food: insects, fruit

Compare: The male Northern Cardinal (p. 285) is larger, with a black mask and red bill. Look for the black wings and tail to help identify the male Scarlet Tanager.

Stan's Notes: A tropical-looking bird. Found in mature deciduous woodlands, where it hunts for insects high up in trees. Requires a territory covering at least 4 acres (1.5 ha) for nesting but prefers 8 acres (3 ha). Arrives late in spring and leaves early in fall. Male and female both sing like American Robins, but the tanagers intersperse an unusual "chick-burr" call in their songs. The song of the female is like that of the male, only softer. This bird is one of hundreds of tanager species in the world. Nearly all are brightly colored and live in the tropics. The name "Tanager" comes from a South American Tupi Indian word meaning "any small, brightly colored bird." The male sheds (molts) his bright-scarlet plumage in the fall, appearing more like the female during winter.

female
p. 147

male

juvenile

YEAR-ROUND

Northern Cardinal
Cardinalis cardinalis

Size: 8–9" (20–23 cm)

Male: Red with a black mask that extends from the face to the throat. Large crest and a large red bill.

Female: buff-brown with a black mask, large reddish bill, and red tinges on the crest and wings

Juvenile: same as female but with a blackish-gray bill

Nest: cup; female builds; 2–3 broods per year

Eggs: 3–4; bluish white with brown markings

Incubation: 12–13 days; female and male incubate

Fledging: 9–10 days; female and male feed the young

Migration: non-migrator

Food: seeds, insects, fruit; comes to seed feeders

Compare: The male Scarlet Tanager (p. 283) is smaller and has black wings. Look for the black mask, large crest, and red bill to identify the male Northern Cardinal.

Stan's Notes: A familiar backyard bird. Seen in a variety of habitats, including parks. Usually likes thick vegetation. One of the few species in which both males and females sing. Can be heard all year. Listen for its "whata-cheer-cheer-cheer" territorial call in spring. Watch for a male feeding a female during courtship. The male also feeds the young of the first brood while the female builds a second nest. Territorial in spring, fighting its own reflection in a window or other reflective surface. Non-territorial in winter, gathering in small flocks of up to 20 birds. *Cardinalis* denotes importance, as represented by the red priestly garments of Catholic cardinals.

female
p. 233

male

Pine Grosbeak
Pinicola enucleator

YEAR-ROUND WINTER

Size: 9" (23 cm)

Male: Plump rose-and-gray finch with a long dark tail. Dark wings smattered with gray. Two white wing bars. Short, pointed dark bill.

Female: mostly gray with dark wings and tail, head and rump have a dull-yellow tinge

Juvenile: male has a touch of red on head and rump; female is similar to the adult female

Nest: cup; female builds; 1 brood per year

Eggs: 4–5; green with small, dark markings

Incubation: 13–15 days; female incubates

Fledging: 13–20 days; female and male feed the young

Migration: irruptive; moves around to find food

Food: seeds, fruit, insects; will come to seed feeders

Compare: Male Purple Finch (p. 281) and male House Finch (p. 279) are much smaller. Look for the gray wings of the male Pine Grosbeak.

Stan's Notes: This winter finch is common in Maine in some years and not so common in others. A very tame and approachable seed eater. Often seen along roads or on the ground, eating tiny grains of sand and dirt, which help aid digestion. Favors coniferous woods, rarely moving out of coniferous regions during summer, but also likes mixed forests. Will bathe in fluffy snow. Flies in a typical finch-like undulating pattern while giving soft, whistle "cheer" calls. Male sings a rich, beautiful song all year long. Male and female develop a pouch in the bottom of their mouths (buccal pouch) during the breeding season for transporting seeds to their young.

in flight

male
p. 273

female

Common Merganser
Mergus merganser

YEAR-ROUND
SUMMER

Size: 26–28" (66–71 cm)

Female: Long, thin, duck-like bird with a rust-red head and ragged "hair." Gray body and white chest and chin. Long, pointed orange bill.

Male: same size and shape as the female, but with a green head, a black back, and white sides

Juvenile: same as female

Nest: cavity; female lines an old woodpecker hole or a natural cavity; 1 brood per year

Eggs: 9–11; ivory without markings

Incubation: 28–33 days; female incubates

Fledging: 70–80 days; female feeds the young

Migration: complete, to southern states and Mexico

Food: small fish, aquatic insects, amphibians

Compare: Female Hooded Merganser (p. 189) has a similar shape, but is much smaller. Hard to confuse with other birds. Look for a rust-red head with ragged "hair," a white chin and a long, pointed, orange bill to identify.

Stan's Notes: Seen on any open water during the winter usually near the coast. A large, shallow-water diver that feeds on fish in 10–15 feet (3–4.5 m) of water. Bill has a fine, serrated-like edge that helps catch slippery fish. Female often lays some eggs in other merganser nests (egg dumping), resulting in up to 15 young in some broods. Male leaves female once she starts incubating. Orphans are accepted by other merganser mothers with young. Fast flight, often low and close to the water, in groups but not in formation.

juvenile

in flight

Arctic Tern
Sterna paradisaea

SUMMER

Size: 12" (30 cm)

Male: White-and-gray tern with a black crown and small dark red bill. Short red legs. Forked tails, seen in flight. Winter plumage has an incomplete black cap and black bill.

Female: same as male

Juvenile: similar to winter plumage adult, scattered brown overall

Nest: ground; female and male construct; 1 brood per year

Eggs: 2; olive with brown markings

Incubation: 20–24 days; female and male incubate

Fledging: 21–28 days; male and female feed young

Migration: complete, to South America

Food: small fish, aquatic insects, insects

Compare: Smaller than the Common Tern (p. 293), which has a larger black-tipped bill.

Stan's Notes: Catches small fish by diving headfirst in water. Nests in large colonies with other terns such as the Common Tern. While most nesting occurs in Canada's Northwest Territories and Alaska, will nest as far south as Maine. Returns to same nest site every year. Vigorously defends nest site and young from predators and people. Long-term relationship between mates. Young stay with the adults during migration to South America.

in flight

Common Tern
Sterna hirundo

SUMMER
MIGRATION

Size: 13–16" (33–40 cm)

Male: White-and-gray tern with a jet-black crown. Red-orange bill with a black tip. Long, forked white "tern" tail. Red legs and feet. Tips of wings appear dark gray when seen in flight.

Female: same as male

Juvenile: similar to adult, with a blue-gray back and white-streaked chest and neck, incomplete brown-to-black crown

Nest: ground; female and male construct; 1 brood per year

Eggs: 1–3; olive-brown with brown markings

Incubation: 21–27 days; female and male incubate

Fledging: 26–27 days; female and male feed young

Migration: complete, to South America

Food: fish, aquatic insects

Compare: Very similar to Arctic Tern (p. 291), but the Common Tern is larger in size and has a larger bill with a black tip. Smaller than Ring-billed Gull (pg. 297) and has a reddish-orange bill and a forked tail. Look for the jet-black crown and the blacktipped red-orange bill to help identify the Common Tern.

Stan's Notes: This tern was nearly eliminated from the state prior to 1900 due to plume hunting. Protected by 1910, it now has made a comeback. Catches small fish by diving into water headfirst. Will catch insects in flight. Arrives at nesting grounds during April. Nest is often in sand or pebbles and lined with grass, shells and aquatic plants. Nests in small colonies. Competition and predation from gulls and birds of prey keep the population from expanding.

breeding

in flight

winter

in flight

Laughing Gull
Leucophaeus atricilla

SUMMER

Size: 16–17" (40–43 cm); up to 3⅓' wingspan

Male: Breeding adult has a black head "hood" and white neck, chest, and belly. Slate-gray back and wings with black wing tips. Orange bill. Incomplete white eye-ring. Winter plumage lacks the "hood" and has a black bill.

Female: same as male

Juvenile: brown throughout, gray sides, lacking the black head and white chest, has a gray bill

Nest: ground; male and female construct; 1 brood per year

Eggs: 2–4; olive with brown markings

Incubation: 18–20 days; female and male incubate

Fledging: 30–35 days; male and female feed young

Migration: complete, to East and Gulf coasts, Mexico, and Central and South America

Food: fish, insects, aquatic insects

Compare: Ring-billed Gull (p. 297) and Herring Gull (p. 299) are larger. Look for the black head "hood" and slate-gray back and wings of the Laughing Gull.

Stan's Notes: This is a three-year gull that starts out mostly brown and gray. The second year it resembles adults but lacks a complete black head "hood." Breeding plumage in the third year. Male tosses its head back and calls to attract a mate. Nests in marshes in large colonies. Nest is a scrape on the ground lined with grass, sticks, and rocks. Adults feed young half-digested food. Name comes from its laughing-like call.

in flight

breeding

juvenile

winter

Ring-billed Gull

Larus delawarensis

YEAR-ROUND
SUMMER

Size: 18–20" (45–51 cm); up to 4' wingspan

Male: White with gray wings, black wing tips spotted with white, and a white tail, seen in flight (inset). Yellow bill with a black ring near the tip. Yellowish legs and feet. In winter, the back of the head and the nape of the neck are speckled brown.

Female: same as male

Juvenile: white with brown speckles and a brown tip of tail; mostly dark bill

Nest: ground; female and male construct; 1 brood per year

Eggs: 2–4; off-white with brown markings

Incubation: 20–21 days; female and male incubate

Fledging: 20–40 days; female and male feed the young

Migration: complete, to coastal Maine and southern coastal states, Mexico

Food: insects, fish; scavenges for food

Compare: Laughing Gull (p. 295) has a black head "hood." The Herring Gull (p. 299) has an orange-red mark on its lower bill and pinkish legs.

Stan's Notes: A common gull of garbage dumps and parking lots. One of the few gulls that winters in Maine. This bird is expanding its range and remaining farther north longer in winter, where it is foraging for food in cities. A three-year gull with different plumages in each of its first three years. Attains the ring on its bill after the first winter and adult plumage in the third year. Defends a small area around the nest, usually only a few feet.

in flight

breeding

juvenile

winter

Herring Gull

Larus argentatus

YEAR-ROUND
SUMMER

Size: 23–26" (58–66 cm); up to 5' wingspan

Male: White with slate-gray wings. Black wing tips with tiny white spots. Yellow bill with an orange-red spot near the tip of the lower bill (mandible). Pinkish legs and feet. Winter plumage has gray speckles on head and neck.

Female: same as male

Juvenile: mottled brown to gray, with a black bill

Nest: ground; female and male construct; 1 brood per year

Eggs: 2–3; olive with brown markings

Incubation: 24–28 days; female and male incubate

Fledging: 35–36 days; female and male feed the young

Migration: complete, to coasts that remain unfrozen in North America; non-migrator in parts of Maine

Food: fish, insects, clams, eggs, baby birds

Compare: Ring-billed Gull (p. 297) is smaller and has yellowish legs and feet and a black ring on its bill. Look for the orange-red spot on the bill to help identify the Herring Gull.

Stan's Notes: A common gull of large lakes. An opportunistic bird, scavenging for human food in dumpsters, parking lots, and other places with garbage. Takes eggs and young from other bird nests. Often drops clams and other shellfish from heights to break the shells and get to the soft interior. Nests in colonies, returning to the same site annually. Lines its nest with grass and seaweed. It takes about four years for the juveniles to obtain adult plumage. Adults have spotted heads during winter.

female

male

in flight

WINTER

Snowy Owl
Bubo scandiacus

Size: 23" (58 cm); up to 4' wingspan

Male: All white with a relatively small round head, bright yellow eyes, and small dark bill. Feet are completely covered with white feathers.

Female: same as male, but dark bar overall

Juvenile: gray with a white face (gray changes later to white), covered with dark horizontal bars, the younger the bird, the more barring

Nest: ground, often in gravel or atop a hummock; 1 brood per year

Eggs: 3–4; white without markings

Incubation: 32–34 days; female incubates

Fledging: 14–20 days; male and female feed the young

Migration: partial to non-migrator, irruptive, to Maine, Canada, and northern states

Food: mammals, birds

Compare: Our only white owl, rarely confused with any other bird.

Stan's Notes: A nesting bird in parts of coastal Maine, known for feeding on lemmings. Moves down through the state in winter in search of food when lemmings aren't plentiful. In some years, may move as far south as northern Texas. The clutch size is dependent on the availability of prey. Prefers to rest on the ground. Male feeds incubating female, but does not incubate. Young hatch several days apart (asynchronously). Families remain together until fall. Often seen on frozen lakes or bays in winter. Blends in with snow. Flies low to the ground on relatively narrow sings with full, stiff wing beats. Shy and unapproachable, unlike many other owls.

in flight

Great Egret
Ardea alba

Size: 36–40" (91–102 cm); up to 4½' wingspan

Male: Tall, thin, all-white bird with a long neck and a long, pointed yellow bill. Black, stilt-like legs and black feet.

Female: same as male

Juvenile: same as adults

Nest: platform; male and female construct; 1 brood per year

Eggs: 2–6; light blue without markings

Incubation: 23–26 days; female and male incubate

Fledging: 43–49 days; female and male feed the young

Migration: complete, to southern coastal states, Mexico, and Central America

Food: small fish, aquatic insects, frogs, crayfish

Compare: Great Blue Heron (p. 263) is similar in shape, but it is larger and gray in color. Look for the long, thin white neck and long, pointed yellow bill to help identify the Great Egret.

Stan's Notes: A graceful, stately bird. Slowly stalks shallow ponds, lakes, and wetlands in search of small fish to spear with its long, sharp bill. Holds neck in an S shape during flight. Nests in colonies with as many as 100 birds. Gives a loud, dry croak if disturbed or when squabbling for a nest site at the colony. The name "Egret" comes from the French word *aigrette*, meaning "ornamental tufts of plumes." The plumes grow near the tail during the breeding season. Hunted to near extinction in the 1800s and early 1900s for its beautiful long plumes, which were used to decorate hats for women. Today, the egret is a protected species.

male

winter
male

female

American Goldfinch
Spinus tristis

YEAR-ROUND

Size: 5" (13 cm)

Male: Canary-yellow finch with a black forehead and tail. Black wings with white wing bars. White rump. No markings on the chest. Winter male is similar to the female.

Female: dull olive-yellow plumage with brown wings; lacks a black forehead

Juvenile: same as female

Nest: cup; female builds; 1 brood per year

Eggs: 4–6; pale blue without markings

Incubation: 10–12 days; female incubates

Fledging: 11–17 days; female and male feed the young

Migration: partial migrator to non-migrator; small flocks of up to 20 birds move around North America; small percentage in Maine will not migrate

Food: seeds, insects; comes to seed feeders

Compare: The male Yellow Warbler (p. 313) is yellow with orange streaks on its chest. The Pine Siskin (p. 107) has a streaked chest and belly and yellow wing bars. The female House Finch (p. 109) and female Purple Finch (p. 121) have heavily streaked chests.

Stan's Notes: Common backyard resident. Most often found in open fields, scrubby areas, and woodlands. Enjoys Nyjer seed in feeders. Breeds in late summer. Lines its nest with the silky down from wild thistle. Almost always in small flocks. Twitters while it flies. Flight is roller coaster-like. Moves around to find adequate food during winter. Often called Wild Canary due to the male's canary-colored plumage. Male sings a pleasant, high-pitched song.

Common Yellowthroat
Geothlypis trichas

SUMMER

Size: 5" (13 cm)

Male: Olive-brown with a bright-yellow throat and chest, a white belly, and a distinctive black mask outlined in white. Long, thin, pointed black bill.

Female: similar to male but lacks a black mask

Juvenile: same as female

Nest: cup; female builds; 2 broods per year

Eggs: 3–5; white with brown markings

Incubation: 11–12 days; female incubates

Fledging: 10–11 days; female and male feed the young

Migration: complete, to southern states, Mexico, and Central America

Food: insects

Compare: The male Yellow Warbler (p. 313) has orange streaking on its chest and no mask. The male American Goldfinch (p. 305) has a black forehead and wings. The Yellow-rumped Warbler (p. 221) only has patches of yellow and lacks the yellow chest of the Yellowthroat.

Stan's Notes: A common warbler of open fields and marshes. Sings a cheerful, well-known "witchity-witchity-witchity-witchity" song from deep within tall grasses. Male sings from prominent perches and while he hunts. He performs a curious courtship display, bouncing in and out of tall grass while singing a mating song. Female builds a nest low to the ground. Young remain dependent on their parents longer than most other warblers. A frequent cowbird host.

male
p. 275

female

American Redstart

Setophaga ruticilla

SUMMER

Size: 5" (13 cm)

Female: Olive-brown warbler with yellow patches on the sides, wings, and tail. White belly.

Male: black with orange patches on the sides, wings and tail; white belly

Juvenile: same as female; male attains orange tinges in the second year

Nest: cup; female builds; 1 brood per year

Eggs: 3–5; off-white with brown markings

Incubation: 12 days; female incubates

Fledging: 9 days; female and male feed the young

Migration: complete, to Mexico, Central America, and South America

Food: insects, seeds, occasionally berries

Compare: The female Yellow-rumped Warbler (p. 221) is similar, but it has a yellow patch on its rump. Look for yellow patches on the sides, wings, and tail to help identify the female Redstart.

Stan's Notes: This is a common and widespread breeding warbler in Maine. Found in woodlands, parks, and yards and at forest edges. Prefers large, unbroken tracts of forest. Appears hyperactive when it feeds, hovering and darting back and forth to glean insects from leaves. Often droops wings and fans tail before launching out to catch an insect. Look for the flashing black-and-orange colors of the male high up in trees. First-year males have yellow markings and look like the females. Sings a high-pitched song that builds in intensity and then suddenly ends.

male

winter male

female

Magnolia Warbler
Setophaga magnolia

Size: 5" (13 cm)

Male: Yellow and black with a gray crown and white eyebrows. Heavy black streaks on a yellow chest and belly. White wing patch. Yellow rump. Obvious white patches on tail.

Female: similar to male but lacks black on the face and has 2 white wing bars

Juvenile: same as female

Nest: cup; female and male build; 1 brood per year

Eggs: 3–5; white with brown markings

Incubation: 11–13 days; female incubates

Fledging: 8–10 days; female and male feed the young

Migration: complete, to Central America

Food: insects

Compare: More yellow than the Yellow-rumped Warbler (p. 221). The Yellow Warbler (p. 313) lacks black on the face and a black back. Palm Warbler (p. 315) has a chestnut cap and thin chestnut streaks on the sides of the breast.

SUMMER

Stan's Notes: A common and widespread warbler in Maine. Can be more abundant during migration, when groups move together. Nests throughout Maine, other northern states, and Canada. Populations are stable due to the ability to adapt to second-growth forest. Look for it low in trees, where it feeds on insects. Often fans its tail while picking insects from the undersides of leaves. Males often feed higher up in trees than the females. Named "Magnolia" when ornithologist Alexander Wilson saw the species for the first time in a magnolia tree.

Yellow Warbler
Setophaga petechia

SUMMER

Size: 5" (13 cm)

Male: Yellow with thin orange streaks on the chest and belly. Long, pointed dark bill.

Female: same as male but lacks orange streaks

Juvenile: similar to female but much duller

Nest: cup; female builds; 1 brood per year

Eggs: 4–5; white with brown markings

Incubation: 11–12 days; female incubates

Fledging: 10–12 days; female and male feed the young

Migration: complete, to southern states, Mexico, and Central and South America

Food: insects

Compare: The Yellow-rumped Warbler (p. 221) has just patches of yellow. The male American Goldfinch (p. 305) has a black forehead and black wings. The female American Goldfinch (p. 305) has white wing bars. Look for the orange streaks on the chest to identify the male Yellow Warbler.

Stan's Notes: A scattered but widespread summer warbler in the state. Seen in shrubby areas close to water, gardens, and back-yards. Zooms around shrubs and shorter trees. A prolific insect eater, gleaning caterpillars and other insects from tree leaves. Male sings loudly, flies off to grab a bug, and then starts singing again. Male sings a string of notes that sound like "sweet, sweet, sweet, I'm-so-sweet!" Seen during migration beginning in August, when birds north of Maine move through the state. Returns in April and May. Males arrive in spring before females to claim ter-ritories. Migrates at night in mixed flocks of warblers. Rests and feeds during the day.

winter

Palm Warbler
Setophaga palmarum

Size: 5½" (14 cm)

Male: Distinctive yellow eyebrows. Yellow throat, belly, and undertail. Obvious chestnut cap. Thin chestnut streaks on the sides of the breast. Dark line across dark eyes.

Female: same as male

Juvenile: same as adults but duller and brown

Nest: cup; female builds; 1–2 broods per year

Eggs: 4–5; white with brown markings

Incubation: 11–12 days; female incubates

Fledging: 12–13 days; female and male feed the young

Migration: complete, to southeastern coastal states, the Caribbean, West Indies and Central America

Food: insects, fruit

Compare: The Yellow-rumped Warbler (p. 221) is similar in size but lacks the yellow throat and belly of the Palm. The Yellow Warbler (p. 313) is slightly smaller and lacks a chestnut cap. Pine Warbler (p. 317) has pronounced white wing bars. Look for the yellow eyebrows and chestnut cap of the Palm Warbler.

Stan's Notes: One of the most common and abundant breeding warblers in the state. Frequently seen in backyard woodlands during migration, when birds north of Maine pass through the state. Look for it to wag or bob its tail while gleaning insects from leaves and flowers of trees. One of the few warblers to feed on the ground. Hops rather than walks. Nests at the edges of northern spruce bogs. Recognizes cowbird eggs and destroys them, burying them with its nest, which it builds on top of the cowbird nest.

Pine Warbler
Setophaga pinus

SUMMER

Size: 5½" (14 cm)

Male: A yellow throat and breast with faint black streaks on sides of breast. Olive-green back. Two white wing bars. White belly.

Female: similar to male, only paler

Juvenile: similar to adults, but is browner with more white on belly

Nest: cup; female builds; 2–3 broods per year

Eggs: 3–5; white with brown markings

Incubation: 10–12 days; female incubates

Fledging: 12–14 days; female and male feed the young

Migration: complete, to southern states

Food: insects, seeds, fruit

Compare: Palm Warbler (p. 315) is similar, but it has a brown cap and yellow eyebrows. Pine Warbler has much more pronounced white wing bars than the Palm Warbler. The Yellow-rumped Warbler (p. 221) has yellow patches on its rump. The American Goldfinch (p. 305) lacks streaks on breast.

Stan's Notes: A common resident of pine forests in the southern two-third of the state. Nests only in pine forest. Brighter in spring and more drab in fall, it varies in color depending upon the time of year. Thought to have a larger bill than the other warblers. Sometimes is easier to identify by its song than by sight. Listen for a twittering, musical song that varies in speed.

female

male
p. 283

Scarlet Tanager
Piranga olivacea

SUMMER

Size: 7" (18 cm)

Female: Drab greenish yellow with olive wings and tail. Whitish wing linings. Dark eyes.

Male: bright scarlet with coal-black wings and tail, an ivory bill and dark eyes

Juvenile: same as female

Nest: cup; female builds; 1 brood per year

Eggs: 4–5; blue-green with brown markings

Incubation: 13–14 days; female incubates

Fledging: 9–11 days; female and male feed the young

Migration: complete, to Central and South America

Food: insects, fruit

Compare: The female Northern Cardinal (p. 147) ha black mask and red bill, but lacks the dark wings of the female Scarlet Tanager. The female Baltimore Oriole (p. 321) has gray-brown wings. The female American Goldfinch (p. 305) has white wing bars.

Stan's Notes: A tropical-looking bird found in mature deciduous woodlands, where it hunts for insects high up in trees. Requires a territory covering at least 4 acres (1.5 ha) for nesting but prefers 8 acres (3 ha). Both the female and male sing like American Robins, but the tanagers intersperse an unusual "chick-burr" call in their songs. The song of the female is like that of the male, only softer. This bird is one of hundreds of tanager species in the world. Nearly all are brightly colored and live in the tropics. The name "Tanager" comes from a South American Tupi Indian word meaning "any small, brightly colored bird." The male sheds (molts) his bright-scarlet plumage in the fall, appearing more like the female during winter.

male
p. 277

female

Baltimore Oriole
Icterus galbula

SUMMER

Size: 7–8" (18–20 cm)

Female: Pale yellow with orange tones and gray-brown wings with white wing bars. Gray bill. Dark eyes.

Male: flaming orange with a black head and back, white-and-orange wing bars, an orange-and-black tail, a gray bill and dark eyes

Juvenile: same as female

Nest: pendulous; female builds; 1 brood per year

Eggs: 4–5; bluish with brown markings

Incubation: 12–14 days; female incubates

Fledging: 12–14 days; female and male feed the young

Migration: complete, to southern states, Mexico, Central America, and South America

Food: insects, fruit, nectar; comes to nectar, orange-half and grape-jelly feeders

Compare: Often confused with the female Scarlet Tanager (p. 319), which has olive-colored wings. Look for the gray-brown wings to identify the female Baltimore Oriole.

Stan's Notes: A fantastic songster, often heard before seen. Easily attracted to bird feeders that offer sugar water (nectar), orange halves, or grape jelly. Parents bring young to feeders. Sits at the top of trees, feeding on caterpillars. Female builds a sock-like nest at the outermost branches of tall trees. Prefers parks, yards, and forests and often returns to the same area year after year. Seen during migration and summer. Some of the last birds to arrive in spring (May) and some of the first to leave in the fall (September). Young males turn orange-and-black at 1½ years of age.

male

female

juvenile

Evening Grosbeak
Coccothraustes vespertinus

YEAR-ROUND
WINTER

Size: 8" (20 cm)

Male: Striking bird with bright-yellow eyebrows, rump, and belly. Black-and-white wings and tail. Dark, dirty-yellow head and large, thick ivory to greenish bill.

Female: similar to male, with softer colors and a gray head and throat

Juvenile: similar to female, with a brown bill

Nest: cup; female builds; 1 brood per year

Eggs: 3–4; blue with brown markings

Incubation: 12–14 days; female incubates

Fledging: 13–14 days; female and male feed the young

Migration: irruptive; moves around the state in winter to find food

Food: seeds, insects, fruit; comes to seed feeders

Compare: The American Goldfinch (p. 305) is closely related, but it is much smaller. The female Pine Grosbeak (p. 233) is slightly larger than the female Evening Grosbeak, and it has a gray head. Look for the yellow eyebrows and thick bill to identify the Evening Grosbeak.

Stan's Notes: One of the largest finches. Characteristic finch-like undulating flight. Uses its unusually large bill to crack seeds, its main food source. Often seen on gravel roads eating gravel, which provides minerals, salt, and grit to grind the seeds it eats. Moves in flocks in winter, searching for food, often visiting feeders. More numerous in some years than others. Population is estimated to have declined more than 80 percent over the past 50 years.

Eastern Meadowlark
Sturnella magna

SUMMER

Size: 9" (23 cm)

Male: Robin-shaped bird with a short tail, yellow chest, and belly; brown back and V-shaped black necklace. White outer tail feathers, best seen when flying away.

Female: same as male

Juvenile: same as adults

Nest: cup on the ground in dense cover; female builds; 2 broods per year

Eggs: 3–5; white with brown markings

Incubation: 13–15 days; female incubates

Fledging: 11–12 days; female and male feed the young

Migration: complete, to southern states, Mexico, and Central America

Food: insects, seeds

Compare: The Horned Lark (p. 133) is smaller and lacks the yellow chest and belly. Look for a V-shaped black marking on the chest to help identify the Eastern Meadowlark.

Stan's Notes: A songbird of open grassy country, singing when perched and in flight. Given the name "Meadowlark" because it's a bird of meadows and sings like the larks of Europe. Best known for its wonderful, clear, flute-like whistling song. Often seen perching on fence posts but will quickly dive into tall grass when approached. Sometimes domes its nest with dried grass. Not in the lark family. A member of the blackbird family, related to grackles and orioles.

BIRDING ON THE INTERNET

Birding online is a great way to discover additional information and learn more about birds. These websites will assist you in your pursuit of birds. Web addresses sometimes change a bit, so if one no longer works, just enter the name of the group into a search engine to track down the new address.

Site	Address
Author Stan Tekiela's homepage	naturesmart.com
American Birding Association	aba.org
Maine Audubon	maineaudubon.org
Cornell Lab of Ornithology	birds.cornell.edu
Maine eBird	ebird.org/atlasme/home
Avian Haven	avianhaven.org
Center for Wildlife	thecenterforwildlife.org

CHECKLIST/INDEX BY SPECIES

Use the boxes to check the birds you've seen.

327

MORE FOR MAINE BY STAN TEKIELA

Identification Guides
Birds of Prey of the Northeast
  Field Guide

Birds of the Northeast

Stan Tekiela's Birding for
  Beginners: Northeast

Children's Books:
Adventure Board Book Series
Floppers & Loppers

Paws & Claws

Peepers & Peekers

Snouts & Sniffers

Children's Books
C is for Cardinal

Can You Count the Critters?

Critter Litter

Children's Books:
Wildlife Picture Books
Baby Bear Discovers the World

The Cutest Critter

Do Beavers Need Blankets?

Hidden Critters

Jump, Little Wood Ducks

Some Babies Are Wild

Super Animal Powers

What Eats That?

Whose Baby Butt?

Whose Butt?

Whose House Is That?

Whose Track Is That?

Nature Books
Bird Trivia

Start Mushrooming

A Year in Nature with Stan Tekie

ABOUT THE AUTHOR

Naturalist, wildlife photographer and writer Stan Tekiela is the originator of the popular state-specific field guide series that includes the *Birds of Massachusetts Field Guide*. Stan has authored more than 190 educational books, including field guides, quick guides, nature books, children's books, and more, presenting many species of animals and plants.

With a Bachelor of Science degree in natural history from the University of Minnesota and as an active professional naturalist for more than 30 years, Stan studies and photographs wildlife throughout the United States and Canada. He has received national and regional awards for his books and photographs and is also a well-known columnist and radio personality. His syndicated column appears in more than 25 newspapers, and his wildlife programs are broadcast on a number of Midwest radio stations. You can follow Stan on Facebook and Twitter or contact him via his website, naturesmart.com.